7th Teaching Innovation & Entrepreneurship Excellence Awards 2021

An Anthology of Case Histories

Edited by Dan Remenyi

7th Teaching Innovation & Entrepreneurship Excellence Awards 2021: An Anthology of Case Histories:

Copyright © 2021 The authors

First published September 2021

All rights reserved. Except for the quotation of short passages for the purposes of critical review, no part of this publication may be reproduced in any material form (including photocopying or storing in any medium by electronic means and whether or not transiently or incidentally to some other use of this publication) without the written permission of the copyright holder except in accordance with the provisions of the Copyright Designs and Patents Act 1988, or under the terms of a licence issued by the Copyright Licensing Agency Ltd, Saffron House, 6-10 Kirby Street, London EC1N 8TS. Applications for the copyright holder's written permission to reproduce any part of this publication should be addressed to the publishers.

Disclaimer: While every effort has been made by the editor, authors and the publishers to ensure that all the material in this book is accurate and correct at the time of going to press, any error made by readers as a result of any of the material, formulae or other information in this book is the sole responsibility of the reader. Readers should be aware that the URLs quoted in the book may change or be damaged by malware between the time of publishing and accessing by readers.

Note to readers: Some papers have been written by authors who use the American form of spelling and some use the British. These two different approaches have been left unchanged.

ISBN 978-1-914587-11-5

Published by: Academic Conferences International, Reading, United Kingdom, info@academic-conferences.org

Available from www.academic-bookshop.com

Table of Contents

Acknowledgements iii
Introduction v
Gaming as an educational tool in entrepreneurial skills, ... 1
  Elizabeth Conradie, Albert Strydom and Ulrich Holzbaur

Military Shark Tank in the Portuguese Military Academy 13
  Corguinho Fernandes

Bringing NPD into the Virtual Classroom: The WORLDSPORT Simulation.. 29
  Keith Goffin, Anna Essén, Mattias Nordqvist and Sebastian Krakowski

Fostering Innovation and Entrepreneurship Skills in Tourism and Hospitality Higher Education: The Case of the Event Management Learning Model.. 49
  Susana Filipa Gonçalves, Ana Gonçalves, Elsa Correia Gavinho, Francisco Silva, Victor Alves Afonso and Cláudia Lopes

Innovation Program for Digital Leaders 63
  Victoria Harrison-Mirauer

Demonstrator Lab: Where Entrepreneurial Academics Become Academic Entrepreneurs 81
  Davide Iannuzzi and Eva C. Janssen

Experiencing Innovation Led by Students................................... 95
  Michal Jirásek and Eva Švandová

Learning Innovation for Enterprise: Skills for the LIFE of an entrepreneurial student.. 107
  Roisin Lyons, Catherine Faherty, Peter Robbins and Philip O'Donnell

Design of a Regional Innovation Ecosystem 123
  Vikram Singh Parmar, Neeraj Sonalkar, Ade Mabogunje, Prafull Anubhai, Larry J Leifer

The Youth Entrepreneurship Summer Program of the Athens University of Economics and Business.. 139
  Katerina Pramatari, Angeliki Karagiannaki, Vasiliki Koniakou and Vasiliki Chronaki

Start-up Lab: An Innovative Entrepreneurship Education Program promoting Students' Start-ups 149
  Alessandra Scroccaro and Alessandro Ross

Promoting Entrepreneurial, Digital and Intercultural Competences with an Interdisciplinary International Virtual Innovation Challenge........ 167
  Audrey Stolze and Gudrun Socher

Acknowledgements

We would like to thank the judges, who initially read the abstracts of the case histories submitted to the competition and discussed these to select those to be submitted as full case histories. These judges will listen to the finalists present their cases at the virtual European Conferences on Innovation and Entrepreneurship supported by Università degli Studi Internazionali di Roma (UNINT) and will select the winner.

We would also like to thank the team of reviewers who performed a double-blind review of the entries and made further selections to produce the finalists who are published in this book.

Dr Christopher Moon FRSA FHEA is a multi-award winning social and eco-entrepreneur with a PhD from Imperial College London. He is the founder of several eco-businesses including eco-design-and-build, eco-taxis and buy-eco. Chris is also inspiring business students at Middlesex University London to be more environmentally friendly. He is widely published including a book for the Economist; and is the inventor developer of the award winning patented eco-bin. Chris was a finalist in the Innovation & Entrepreneurship Teaching Excellence Awards 2015. He is a psychologist by background; certified and accredited CSR consultant and Social Auditor.

Dr Ken Grant is a professor of entrepreneurship and strategy in the Ted Rogers School of Business Management He is a visiting professor in the UK, Europe and Asia. His research interests include strategy, entrepreneurship, knowledge management and innovation, and pedagogy. He is an active coach and supporter of student entrepreneur activity across the university and is currently working to facilitate the development of entrepreneurship programs in China. Prior to joining Ryerson, Dr. Grant had an extensive career as a management consultant and industry executive in Canada and the UK, leading global consulting practices in several major firms.

He holds a BA degree from the Open University, an MBA from the Schulich School of Business and a DBA from Henley Business School.

Christy Suciu completed her graduate degree at Webster University and teaches in the College of Business and Economics at Boise State University in the area of design thinking, innovation, and strategy. She has created all three design thinking and strategy courses in the different M.B.A. programs. Over the years she has served as a design thinking consultant for many major companies such as HP, Wells Fargo, Paksense, and Biomark. Her research has been published in the Academy of Management Learning and Education and titled, "The need for Design Thinking in Business Schools".

Introduction

Today more than ever Innovation and entrepreneurship skills are desired by both individuals starting out on new business endeavours and to employers. But there has always been an issue surrounding how to teach and learn these skills. Some universities offer degrees or other courses in these subjects, whilst others incorporate these topics in a variety of different degrees. But whatever approach the university takes these topics are quite challenging to teach, and also difficult to research. Courses and modules on these subjects are often quite theoretical and often they neither deliver the practical knowhow required nor do they inspire our students to become innovators or entrepreneurs. Fortunately, some good work is being done in this field in various parts of the world and this annual competition highlights such initiatives.

The response this year to the 7th Teaching Innovation and Entrepreneurship Excellence Awards has reflected the innovative initiatives in place in many parts of the world. With 30 initial submissions, 20 competitors were invited to send in a full case history describing their initiative. The range of subjects written about in the case histories has certainly been extensive and the panel of reviewers had their job cut out for them to find the most interesting case histories and short list them to the finalists published in this anthology. 12 authors or groups of authors have been invited to present their work at the virtual European Conference on Innovation and Entrepreneurship supported by Università degli Studi Internazionali di Roma (UNINT). The topics which will be addressed are listed in the Contents page of this book.

I would like to thank all the contributors to this book for the excellent work which has been done towards developing new and interesting ways of teaching Innovation and Entrepreneurship. And of course, it is also important to thank the individuals who constituted our panel of reviewers and expert judges.

Dan Remenyi PhD
Editor

Gaming as an educational tool in entrepreneurial skills,

Elizabeth Conradie[1], Albert Strydom[2] and Ulrich Holzbaur[3]
[1]Idea Generator Unit (*i*-GYM), Central University of Technology, Free State, South Africa
[2]-Faculty of Management Sciences, Central University of Technology, Free State, South Africa
[3]Department of Management Sciences, Aalen University of Applied Sciences, Aalen, Germany.
econradie@cut.ac.za

1. Introduction

Innovation and Entrepreneurship Teaching Initiative: Conceptualization, development, deployment and evaluation of an entrepreneurial game to teach economic principles with a focus on what is needed to establish a sustainable enterprise initiative with the aim to teach entrepreneurial economic principles to a diverse target audience that includes unemployed persons; potential entrepreneurs and those entrepreneurs running small enterprises; learners in primary and secondary education as well as students and academics that should be transformed towards entrepreneurship are presented for the award.

The basic aim with the development of the game was to introduce entrepreneurship in a practical and visible way to the target markets mentioned above. The big picture with the development of the game is to contribute to socio-economic sustainable development through job creation in South Africa, also globally, although the initial implementation did take place in the Free State Province, in central South Africa. In the wake of - relative high unemployment coupled with a lack of entrepreneurial skills, entrepreneurial education- and training in the Free State Province, as well is in the broader South African context, - became imperative (Free State Growth and Development Strategy, 2014). -A similar sentiment exists in Europe. Underrepresented within the entrepreneurial population and especially founders of start-ups are young people, women, disabled people and/or migrants. The following quote from the European Union 2020 Action Plan is very applicable given the current scenario: "Establish and run entrepreneurship education schemes for the unemployed to enable them to (re-)enter business life as entrepreneurs ...in partnership with education and training systems as an engagement route into second chance education" (EU 2020 ACTION PLAN Reigniting the entrepreneurial spirit in Europe).

Against the abovementioned background the following question arises: Why utilizing educational games in entrepreneurship? The answer lies in the fact that gaming is social interactive and a constructive way to gain knowledge in a fun way which underlines a critical and reflective method of learning and to consolidate course knowledge (Chan et al, 2017). "It's the act of problem solving that makes games so engaging" MacKenty (2006: 46-48). Game play is productive in solving problems and sharing solutions, to develop, to test, and share strategies (Games, Learning, and Society group, 2005/2007).

An educational game has features that facilitate learning such as the participants can take on a new identity; interactivity as they perform an action to get feedback; they learn by doing; playing allows them to learn from failure, while the content can be scaffolded into well-ordered problems -(Smale, 2011: 36-55).

Fox, Pittaway and Uzuegbunam (2018: 61-89) stated that as many games do not -engage the learner into deeper critical reflection, instructor engagement in the classroom may somewhat alleviate this problem. Development of the Valu-E game process included this factor -and it is offered as a facilitated group activity with elements of the traditional teaching methods as the instructor still plays an authoritative role.

2. The infrastructure of the game

The game was developed in various stages starting with discussions between Aalen University of Applied Sciences in Germany and the Faculty of Management Sciences (FMS) of the Central University of Technology (CUT), Free State in South Africa. The initial basic game (Vogelsang, 2008) was designed for education in schools to train participants in basic economic knowledge and elementary bookkeeping concepts.

The idea for the VALYU game came up during various projects -at CUT and especially the Product Development Technical Station-at CUT, -in the process of providing support to local communities and entrepreneurs. The project teams realized that not only technology, but also economic knowledge and entrepreneurial attitude, were necessary to create jobs and fight unemployment. The teams also realized that various levels were necessary to become a successful sustainable entrepreneur. The first version of the game under the name "micro-econ-nomy" was developed at Aalen University and was intended to teach basic business principles. This became level one and two of the game and was tested, evaluated and improved in various schools and the two universities. Games for project management and leadership which were already in use at Aalen university were adapted to become level four. A focus was -placed on sustainability adaptation of various games and puzzles to become level five. Some levels were jointly developed by the team and CUT -colleagues to give the participants marketing skills and the attitude to do the final step-of business plan development.

The board game set was then developed in a in multi-level game to include basic economics, accounting, marketing, sustainability management and the compilation of a business plan for a wider audience. Throughout the whole development phase, training and train-the-trainer seminars have been used to create impacts and to evaluate and improve the game set. The game design was tested to provide design information for the development of other educational gaming tools to teach similar diverse groups. The nature of teaching was to utilize a social interactive facilitated educational game constructed in such a way that participants exchange information with both instructor and other participants, gaining knowledge in a fun way.

The initial development of the game was done by selected staff members of FMS under the leadership of Prof Uli Holzbaur of Aalen University and Prof Albert Strydom of CUT. Initial VAL-U game sessions for assessment were facilitated by Dr Edem Agbobli, students of CUT and students of Aalen University of Applied Sciences.

In 2017 to 2019 the game was developed into a fully fledge board game- (VALU-E®) by an innovator at - CUT- facilitated by the Idea Generator Unit (*i*-GYM) Innovation Services for Innovation and Entrepreneurship Advancement and the Faculty of Management Sciences at CUT to be rolled out as a commercial enterprise. These developments and extensive refining of the VALU-E game which included the physical game board design and prototyping of the board with additional add-ons was done by innovator Mr. Marnus van Zyl. This development to refine of the game was facilitated through playing different levels of the game -during several sessions with a variety of participants e.g., students of different year groups, community members, learners and staff members at the Idea Generator Unit (*i*-GYM), CUT. The content of the different levels is listed in Table 1.

Table 1: Entrepreneurship content of the Valu-E levels

Sustainable development, Corporate social responsibility, Environmental Awareness
Business plan development, Identifying key aspects of the business plan
Taking individual responsibly, Patience and Perseverance
Marketing and Sales, Risk management, Supply & Demand, Quality & Research
Accounting, cost analysis, interest & taxes, investment & financing
Concept of value creation, elementary economics
Leadership and teamwork, company vision and mission

The VALU-E Game is accompanied by a comprehensive manual which describes the learning outcomes of the game as well as the fundamentals behind it.

The VALU-E Game explains the basics of entrepreneurship to any learner who is not knowledgeable in this regard. Therefore, it is transferrable to a variety of settings as teaching method: it is applicable on all age groups, disciplines, cultures, genders, etc. The emphasis is on the establishment of entrepreneurial values, strategies, adding monetary value, creating value for any customer, dealing with customers, employees and other stakeholders with various cultural backgrounds, age groups, etc.

During evaluation sessions of the different levels of the game in training sessions with a variety of groups, the additional add-on activities were evaluated. These VALU-E game sessions for assessment were facilitated by Mr. Marnus van Zyl, assisted by i-GYM assistants, Me Laurentia Klassen and Me Itumeleng Mohapi. The VALU-E game is now fully developed for face-to-face delivery under the leadership of a facilitator. Intellectual Property belongs to CUT and two inventors.

3. The challenges

The basic challenge is to make entrepreneurship education interesting to learners with various backgrounds from elementary school learners to senior people who want to start a business, and from engineers to people without any formal education. The game addresses a variety of target groups in a huge variety of contexts. The training units should be general enough to be modified and adapted.

While the rollout at CUT was quite uncomplicated involving various staff members and students, the goal of a nation-wide rollout faces financial and organizational challenges.

Feedback received from participants of the VALU-E Game indicates an overwhelming positive response in terms of the instrument being able to correspond to the learning outcomes associated to it. This confirms the validity aspect. Although participants varied in terms of age, gender and/or race the same results were achieved over time, which is an indication of the reliable nature of the game.

Positive feedback was received from all participants who were trained in the basics of entrepreneurship through the game set. Learning outcomes were measured with feedback surveys and the information gained were used to improve and adapt the game during evaluation sessions. Most participants indicated that it was a fun experience through which they gained new decision directed knowledge, letting them feel more confident to do business. The game was used in various settings such as in the initial phase: farmers; in the mining industry; unemployed members of the community; and in the second phase primary school learners; secondary school learners; unemployed members of the community, students and university staff members.

The following groups were evaluated:

Local school – learners

Group profile: Age 17-18 years

Date: 2017

Outcomes: No formal feedback was done for learner group however the overwhelming response was positive as all learners indicate they want to attend more sessions. Difficulty level of games could easily be adapted by the facilitator, however a trained assistant for every ten participants was essential and this was implemented.

Small Business & Management Sciences Student Groups

Group profile: Small test groups of Accounting Students for specific game levels

Date: 2017

Some of students did not experience-the accounting game as 'challenging enough' and an auditing level had to be incorporated to keep interest going. This led to the addition of 'red alert' questions added to ensure interest and active discussions during the game. 'Red alert' questions added to the knowledge gain and was linked with concepts taught -through formal educational instruction.

Management Sciences Executive group

Group profile: Lecturers

Date: January 2018

Positive response after playing three of the levels of the game lead to the approval for the implementation of the VALU-E game for training of Management Science students hosted at the Idea Generator Unit (*i*-GYM), CUT to facilitate student's entrepreneurship education during normal educational programme. Lectures see implementation in the curriculum as possible except for the time factor as session needs 1.5 – 2 hours.

Management and Business Science Students

Group profile: Management and Business Science Students in a classroom setting; groups size of 40-45 participants per session, total of ~ 300 students over a period of 10 months.

Date: February to October 2018

Most participants indicated it was a fun experience, learning entrepreneurial skills and that they gain new decision directed knowledge playing the game and indicated that playing the game let them feel more confident to do business.

Community Group, Heidedal, Mangaung, FS

Group profile: Unemployed persons interested in entrepreneurship

Date: March 2019

Feedback from a group of 15 unemployed participants with an education profile that include six participants with previous training in business studies: four participants did business / accounting studies at school level and two participants studied business training at a higher education level. All participants indicate that they would like to own and manage their own business. Unedited answers after playing the Micro economy and Accounting game levels were as follows:

Do you feel that you learned something new?

> *"Teamwork, patience, partnership goes a long way; **you need to take risks**; also, to spend money wisely in order to make a profit; learn that accuracy is very important"*

> *"I have learned the difference between skill needed to purchase a business compared to start up a business; I learned the "complications of money"*

Suggestion on how to improve the session(s):

> *"More sessions; all was well put together; it was very good to learn about business planning; everything was perfect; everything was perfect; no suggestion, everything was perfect; not really – it is good; everything was fine; we need more time to continue."*

Were you at any point in the game, reminded of a concept that you have previously learned or experienced?

> *"You have to double check the figures all the time - had my own business, just learned the importance of it and why certain things didn't work out"*

The VALU-E game created interest among participants to start their own businesses and in the process enhancing socio-economic development. Lessons learnt in the game design process is that the training must match the requirements of the target groups as participants come from different backgrounds and a varied profile of previous education or exposure to business.

4. Learning outcomes

The sessions provided design information for the development of other educational gaming tools and improving on the game levels. It was observed that the game can be adapted by a well-trained facilitator and assistants to be an effective educational tool for different educational levels and business experience. In a facilitated game the instructor can react on the group dynamics during a session and adapt the game to the specific situation. Observation of assistants & facilitators do have value and can improve outcomes during training, as well invaluable post game feedback to improve game development. The 2019 study did not include a follow-up survey of the participants and whether the training -promoted start-ups. The aim of the 2021 intervention was to keep track of the progress and challenges encountered. To evaluate the outcomes of Valu-E training other than creating an interest in entrepreneurship a session was to again provide community members the opportunity to play some of the educational games and also at the same day attend traditional training workshops in entrepreneurship development - workshops that form part of a formalize online formal entrepreneurship development program (EDP) program on offer for free by the i-GYM Unit, CUT innovation Services.

Some of the outcomes of this ongoing comparative study is as follow:

Community Group, Heidedal, Mangaung, FS

Group profile: Persons interested in entrepreneurship and most planning to start a business or already in busines, an initiative facilitated by Me Laurentia Klasssen, i-GYM assistant.

Date: March/ April 2021

Responses after Valu-E game sessions hosted for community members (interested in entrepreneurship or in business already) in combination with more traditional pedagogical teaching entrepreneurship workshop was based on the following statement:'Valu-E game or EDP workshops? Direct quotations from participants in response were as follows:

"EDP is more informative"

"The Valu-E game is more practical"

"Both educational however I learnt more through EDP"

"The Valu-E game helps more with specific business although EDP is more informative"

"The Valu-E game is a fun and relaxing way to learn"

"Attending both was fruitful…learnt a lot in a short period of time — things I did not realize I would need"

The results indicated than an interest was created by attending the Valu-E game in combination with EDP workshops and furthermore lead to sign-up of 6 of the 15 participants for the full formal entrepreneurship development program. The outcome of this participation will be evaluated at the end of this program again with a combined Valu-E and EDP session.

Observations from instructors was that the game taught participants to become more supportive of each other in their group in gaining knowledge due to the competitive nature of this gaming teaching method.

Resistance to implement gaming as an educational tool is due to the lecture's choice of resources and methods due to factors as listed by Riccio, Sakata and Carastan (2000, ppp1962-1999), e.g. preparation time, knowledge of the method, characteristics of the group and incentive from the institution do play a role.

The primary learning outcome of the game is to create entrepreneurship awareness amongst trainees in the various target markets in the following areas: Elementary economics; Basic accounting; Marketing principles; Sustainable development; Strategic management, and Compilation of a business plan. The secondary learning outcome is to enable trainees to set-up a basic business through knowledge gained through the achievement of the learning outcomes mentioned above.

5. Further development

Investigations are underway to see how the game can be included in the core curriculum on offer at CUT. If that can be achieve it will be compulsory for all students of CUT to be exposed to the game during their study careers. Such a step will fit perfectly to CUT's objective to become an entrepreneurial university of note in Central South Africa. The game will also play a central role as one of the core activities of the recently approved Unit for Entrepreneurship Development at CUT. Universities' strategic drive to become true entrepreneurial universities is essential to change attitudes towards promoting entrepreneurship / starting a business among students and staff - offering incentives to the facilitators and student participants are crucial.

The game will also be continuously improved and adapted for various scenarios from school to university and from small scale business to technical start-ups. The game will be adapted to additional target groups, and professional and pedagogical contexts. Future project initiatives aim to approach corporates (also as part of their Corporate Social Responsibility), chambers of commerce, government institutions and the Department of Education in the Free State Province of South Africa to co-partner with the roll-out of the game. Dr Johan van Zyl, a Senior Researcher and marketing expert in FMS, is currently in the process to develop a marketing plan to support this process as well a consultant employed by CUT Innovation Services to look for the optimal commercialisation route. The current commercialization process of the VALU-E game may provide evidence that gaming can be both educational as well as a business venture. The aim is to distribute and deploy the game all over South Africa and globally to improve entrepreneurial education and to create jobs and businesses for all ages.

The idea is also to investigate options to market and implement the game on the online platform in future. With the digitalization of some levels in the game as was found by adding competitive game elements in online operating system courses by Lai et al (2012), it will increase the level of attraction of courses to students, they will be willing to spend time because they want to win, thus fulfilling the purpose of elevating learning motivation. Applying new technologies to some of the levels will facilitate access for other target groups that can benefit from this educational multi-level entrepreneurial game.

Note: This work was presented at the 15th European Conference on Innovation and Entrepreneurship (ECIE20), Università degli Studi Internazionali di Roma (UNINT), Rome, Italy ,17th-18th September 2020 (Conradie, Strydom and Holzbaur, 2020).

References

Chan, K.Y.G., Tan, S.L., Hew, K.F.T. et al. (2017), 'Knowledge for games, games for knowledge: designing a digital roll-and-move board game for a law of torts class', *RPTEL* 12(7) [online] Available at: https://doi.org/10.1186/s41039-016-0045-1

Conradie, E., Strydom, A., & Holzbaur, U. (2020), 'Gaming as an educational tool to teach entrepreneurial skills', In: *ECIE 2020 16th European conference on innovation and entrepreneurship, Academic Conferences Limited*, p177.

Entrepreneurship 2020 Action Plan, (2020), 'Reigniting the entrepreneurial spirit in Europe', *COMMUNICATION FROM THE COMMISSION TO THE EUROPEAN PARLIAMENT, THE COUNCIL, THE EUROPEAN ECONOMIC AND SOCIAL COMMITTEE AND THE COMMITTEE OF THE REGIONS*.

Fox J., Pittaway L., Uzuegbunam I. (2018), 'Simulations in Entrepreneurship Education: Serious Games and Learning Through Play', *Entrepreneurship Education and Pedagogy*. 1 (1), p61-89.

Free State Growth and Development Strategy (2014), Available at http://app.spisys.gov.za/files/pula/topics/3037832/Provincial_Strategies/Free_State_Province/file_84516279.

Games, Learning, and Society group (2005/2007), *Proceedings of_the_Games_Learning_Society_Conference,* 3. [online] Available at: https://www.academia.edu/8692640/

Lai, C-H., Lee, T-P., Jong, B-S., *et al*. (2012), 'A Research on Applying Game-Based Learning to Enhance the Participation of Student'. In: Park J., Jeong YS., Park S., Chen HC. (eds) Embedded and Multimedia Computing Technology and Service. *Lecture Notes in Electrical Engineering, Springer, Dordrecht*, 181.

MacKenty, B. (2006), 'All Play and No Work.' *School Library Journal*, 52, p46-48.

Riccio, E.L., Sakata, M.C.G and Carastan, J. (2000), 'Teaching – learning methods in accounting education – an empirical research in the Brazillian scenario.' *Accounting* Research in Brazilian Universities.Caderno de Estudos, p1962-1999.

Smale, M. A. (2011) 'Learning through quests and contests: Games in information literacy instruction.', *Journal of Library Innovation*, 2(2), p36-55.

Vogelsang, M. (2008) 'Konzeption und Implementierung eines einfachen und kulturübergreifenden Planspiels zur Einführung in die Grundlagen der Betriebswirtschaft.', *Diplomarbeit. Aalen: Hochschule Aalen*.

Author Biographies

Dr Elizabeth Conradie is a manager at the Idea Generator Unit, Central University of Technology, Free State, South Africa (SA). She received her PhD in Molecular Biology from University of Stellenbosch, SA. She is currently working the field of entrepreneurship and innovation. Her main research areas are new enterprise and training developments with an interest in gamification as an educational tool.

Prof. Albert Strydom is the dean of the Faculty of Management Sciences at the Central University of Technology, Free State (CUT), SA. His research speciality is Tourism and Hospitality Management in Marketing – especially from an entrepreneurial perspective. He played a major role in the management of the development process to establish the VALU-E Game.

Dr Ulrich Holzbaur studied Mathematics and worked in Operations Research at Ulm University and in systems development in industry. His lectures and research at Aalen University, Germany comprise sustainable development, project management and mathematical modelling. In education, he makes wide use of projects and games. Holzbaur is head of the Steinbeis Centre on Applied Management, and honorary professor at CUT.

Military Shark Tank in the Portuguese Military Academy

Corguinho Fernandes
Centro de Investigação Desenvolvimento e Inovação da Academia Militar, Academia Militar, Instituto Universitário Militar, Lisbon, Portugal
helio.fernandes@academiamilitar.pt

Abstract: This paper aims to overview the innovation and entrepreneurship teaching process in the Portuguese Military Academy. The evolution of the methods and the impact indicators are presented. The evolution of 6 editions of the entrepreneurship program named Military Shark Tanks is reviewed, and the projection to future goals is made with the attention given in European and overseas enlargement. Military entrepreneurship education and mainly senior entrepreneurship by veterans is reviewed. The novelty of the work is in the case study of Military Shark Tanks contributes to innovation and entrepreneurship learning. Policies can be applied to prepare better the future of Military Administration Cadets: leaders responsible for managing financial, human, and material resources.

1. Introduction

The combination of entrepreneurship and military are not usually in the same sentence. The relationship of the entrepreneurial activity with innovation and business is essentially a matter of the private sector, far away from the military personal of the Armed Forces. However, there is a point, and usually, it happens earlier than with civilians: retirement, when the particular skills of leadership, resilience, and organisation can be adapted.

The academic research about senior entrepreneurship is confined to developed countries, where it is more usual to became an entrepreneur by opportunity than in developing countries, where necessity is the primary determinant (Ács et al., 2004; Zhao et al., 2012). In civilian and generic terms, senior entrepreneurship is the practise whereby individuals aged 50+ participate in ventures. The pursue of active ageing, non-monetary self-rewards and extending working lives through entrepreneurship are described for several OCDE countries (Figueiredo & Paiva, 2019; Maritz,

2015; Matos et al., 2018; Saiz-Álvarez & Coduras-Martínez, 2020; Soto-Simeone & Kautonen, 2020).

In the new condition of a retired military veteran, the incursion in a venture is studied by academics like Smaliukienė (2013), highlighting the need to provide more entrepreneurial skills in military career to prepare for early retired servicemen. The links between military formation and its revenue in the retirement age has been studied by Crecente et al. (2021) and concludes that mandatory military service, where essential skills to entrepreneurial activity are developed, does not predispose to start-up creation. In the perspective of a long career in the Armed Forces, the statement that in the military career, the skills practised and acquired represent a good chance of surviving and better adapt as an entrepreneur in the retirement period is highly criticised by Chukwu (2021). The author argues that military training may not ensure entrepreneurial success and the military condition can negatively impact and became an inhibiting factor.

In developing countries, the study cases and research around the senior-military-entrepreneurship in countries like Nigeria are well stated by Lawan (2021) and Ojo and Fakokunde (2021). Their suggestions to mitigate the tension between military culture and entrepreneurship culture relies upon more institutional support to allow transference of military skills and develop the information and communication technology skills, which are not so developed during the military career.

Despite some studies about the senior entrepreneurship of veterans, there is no data about the impact of teaching entrepreneurship skills to Cadets that will become Officers. As Água and Correia (2021) stated, military leaders belonging to the category of Officer in the Armed Forces have the responsibility of manage most of the resources: financial, human, physical means and time. Therefore, military academies should be the starting point of theory and practice of developing a business blueprint and implement it.

Research about teaching entrepreneurial technics to MBA/management students are well documented by Lotulung et al. (2018), with critics to the lecture process as the only one to teach the ability to become an entrepreneur. The author presents the method Contextual Teaching Learning as a solution with which the Military Shark Tank can be aligned. In a different but complementary way, Karlan and Valdivia (2011) reported the impact of teaching entrepreneurship to actual entrepreneurs. As the reality of business worldwide is made of non-ex-students of management, the author evaluated the results of business training to a Peruvian group of female entrepreneurs dependent on microfinance credit. However, the results were unsatisfactory: there is little or no evidence that entrepreneurs involved in the training process get more revenue due to the newly learned skills.

This article plunges into the experience of a Military Administration Cadet of the Portuguese Army and Republican National Guard (GNR) to create and implement a project idea with application in the Portuguese Military Academy. The contribution of the research & development (R&D) centre and the role of the Academy in the Portuguese Army and the GNR is explained in the first section. Next is explained the evolution of the case study of this article, followed by the presentation of the five stages of the Military Shark Tank process. In section four are shown the most successful winners of the program in recent years. In the end, are submitted some recommendations for future applications and maximisations of this teaching program.

1.1 Between the hierarchy, there is an Academy

The openness of the mind for a Cadet of Military Administration is gradual but fast: the final output after five years in the Military Academy is an Officer prepared to advise in the financial and budgetary management.

After two and a half years of Academy, the propensity to criticise positively is high. However, the access and knowledge of the tools that can mitigate the gaps, enhance the human and physical framework, or increase institutional notoriety are naturally limited.

The military version of Shark Tank, or simply the application of entrepreneurship tools in the students of Military Administration, has the same challenges: ignorance of the potential installed on campus and in the institution.

1.2 In the Military Academy, one can find:
- R&D centre with more than 15 years and almost 100 researchers from the Portuguese Army and various researchers contributing to the military sciences.
- Three competence centres in military fields: Leadership, Ballistic and Infrastructures Protection.
- Laboratories linked to engineering areas.

- Several links/protocols with public institutions surround the campus of Lisbon and Amadora.

There is a real need to rapidly incentivise the Cadet to search for the institution's possibilities to respond to the necessities of the students and personal that works there.

To improve the Cadets' performance, after they present the initial ideas of projects they are interested in exploring, the nomination of experts in the institution aims to maximise, reject, or reformulate the idea.

2. The Innovation: get a feasible idea!

Since 2014, six editions have been logistically supported by the Military Academy's TV studio in Amadora Campus for recording and multimedia editing. In the last seven years, Military Shark Tank has evolved from a presentation of general ideas of entrepreneurship and investment analysis to the actual shape in the TV Studio with 1.500€ of budget granted by the Military Academy to implement the winner idea.

In the first years of the subject, this exercise of project planning was mere theory. Students were invited to develop an idea defined by the teachers, with applicability to the civil sector, in a group and present the hypothetical challenges during the stages from study the idea to the final stage of control/monitoring the project. During the evaluation of the subject, the idea evolved to the hypothetical implementation in the military sector.

After this experiment the year after, the evaluation turned that it could be even better if we work for good: real challenges with real resources for real people!

Since 2018, the Commander and Chief of the Military Academy is approving the enhancement of this event, which increased the motivation exponentially: a single Cadet can be responsible for the change of life of hundreds of comrades for a very long time!

One of the pillars of the formation in the Military Academy is the need to strengthen leadership skills: auto control, idea projection, speed of discernment or judgment. All these characteristics are tested before a jury composed of the General responsible for the Teaching Area and other experts. Later, the visualisation of an edited video allows the analysis of the behaviour and response to the project's critics presented.

All this performance and ex-post analysis are possible because the Military Academy invests permanently in a TV studio with excellent resources and continuous personal formation. Figures 1 to 3 are representative of the available resources to promote and enhance the event:

Figure 1: - Interior of the TV studio: "Sharks" Panel

Figure 2: Interior of the TV studio: overall picture

A video is edited to promote this event in social media where Military Academy is active: Website, Facebook, Instagram and YouTube.

Figure 3: Frame from the 3rd edition of Military Shark Tank

3. Military Shark Tank: The Overall Process

Within the scope of Investment Analysis subject of the master course in Military Administration at the Military Academy, students are invited to present investment projects with military applicability to complement the theory of business plan, blueprint or financial plans.

A multidisciplinary jury is responsible for evaluating the originality, relevance, feasibility, and budget asked the Military Academy Commander (to implement the project) in Shark Tank's reality show format. The objective is to present an investment idea to obtain gains by generating revenue, reducing costs, or increasing the military institution's notoriety.

Figure 4 shows the five stages that configure an adaptation to projects real life cycle:

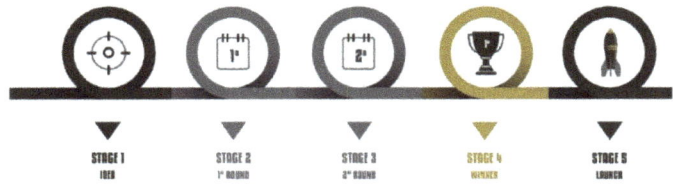

Figure 4: Stages of Military Shark Tank

Stage 1 – Idea definition. The scope is limited to the application in the Military Academy Campus of Lisbon and Amadora. Both campuses combined are a rich field where more than 200 people contribute to forming the new Officers of the Portuguese Army and the GNR, Portuguese Speaking Countries and of course, where almost 400 Cadets live, study and socialise 24 under 24 hours a day.

The area includes 36ha in Amadora and 8ha in Lisbon, with a diversity of buildings, infrastructures, landscapes, utilities, and services that can be maximised to improve the Cadet quality of study and life.

Stage 2 – In the first round, all Cadets present their project ideas in the classroom to the responsible teachers. Teachers classify the ideas and also receive the student's feedback to evaluate through a hetero evaluation.

This stage occurs in the classroom with standard hardware; however, depending on the type of project, Cadets are invited to be innovators and present actual output or a prototype of their idea.

Stage 3 – The three best ideas are presented to a panel of specialists and Commanders – "sharks" in the TV studio, simulating a judgment environment under pressure. Not only by the "sharks" but also by the cameras, lights and all scenography!

Stage 4 – The choice of the best project(s) and the one(s) considered with more conditions will be presented to the Commander in Chief to be implemented in the Military Academy. In general, if the best-classified project does not overpass the budget, other project ideas from the top 3 are invited to be implemented.

Stage 5 – Implementation in the Military Academy means the exploration stage in a very peculiar environment: the defence and public sectors.

The restrictions to the private sector to provide services to the defence sector are very common, which shrinks the universe of companies available to implement critical services and solutions. The confidentiality could increase the difficulty of implementing a project or delay the implementation until access to the Portuguese Armed Forces is granted.

Procurement and access to the Portuguese State budget during the year (without previous provision planned in the year before) increases the difficulty of hiring private services/goods. The legislation applicable to the public sector is also very rigorous to accomplish that the public contracts use with efficiency the endowment of the Military Academy, which means the Portuguese money collected mainly from the taxes.

4. The learning outcomes

4.1 Walk-in someone else's shoes: Being an entrepreneur of "my" mind!

In the first years of Military Shark Tank, it was planned to occur at the end of the semester, so theory about a project evaluation and implementation could influence the output of the ideas/projects.

COVID-19 lived during the second semester of 2020, forced to assume the Military Shark Tank at the beginning of the semester. The results were even better: the examples used in class during the teaching of the stages and the analysis of an idea were no longer theoretic, but the concrete situation lived by each student. The evidence that the actual situation lived by each "entrepreneur" turned in more motivations, better comprehension and changed the way the students look to the exercises of project evaluation.

Military Shark Tank is now an essential bridge to jump from theory to practice, from books to the daily life that an Administration Officer will be forced to respond to, finding solutions from a minimal budget to ensure the mission is still accomplished.

4.2 They did it: Good examples of thinking for the community with low resources

Academia de Pensadores – Thinkers Academy

The concept is straightforward: a room, two institutions and a group of cadets willing to express their opinion. The project aims to create a space for debate where, based on a theme, Cadets can, through a previously defined debate model, present their ideas in a brainstorming format, after which a debate follows to achieve or some final ideas. As shown by Figure 5, the final objective is to work on the final ideas to present them superiorly or present them in the context of an amphitheatre with an audience. The project aims to develop the critical spirit and orality of the students and make them grow as military citizens and politicians.

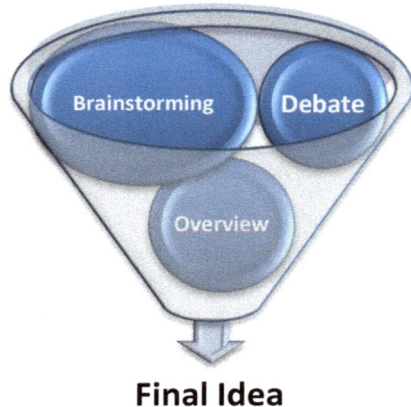

Figure 5: Process of "Thinkers Academy" project

It is essential to realise that, by law, the military is obliged to be non-partisan; however, this does not imply that he is non-political. In other words, the military can express its opinion on a topic, be it of a political, economic or social nature. The themes chosen for the sessions must meet the interests of both the Army and the GNR. Therefore, the typology and scope of the chosen themes can be either economic (Example: financial crises), political (Ex: armed conflicts), social (Ex: domestic violence) or another topic of interest to the Military Academy. A moderating team will moderate the sessions, and multiannual teams that defend their idea in a debate entered the debate. In the end, the best ones are chosen for later presentation.

5. Electronic Dispensation Map

The Electronic Dispensation Map is a platform attached to the Internal Academic website that will allow the scheduling and management of the Cadets dismissals – authorisation to leave the headquarter or miss the meals.

This project has as main objective to promote the efficiency and effectiveness of the marking system of dismissals implemented in the Military Academy.

The system will be equipped with three types of users, as demonstrated by Figure 6:

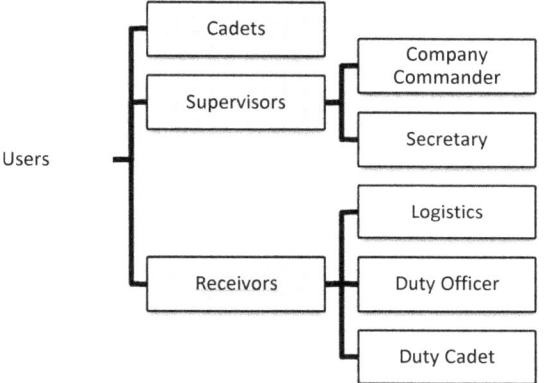

Figure 6: Overview of data users of "Electronic Dispensation Map" project

a. Cadets:
- They will be able to edit the appointment of their dismissals, having to do so based on the internal regulation.
- Upon accessing the platform, they will be able to observe the map in its entirety, including the dismissals of the remaining Cadets of the Company.

b. Supervisors:
- They will have the ability to edit Cadet dismissals at any time.
- Authorise the dismissals maps.

c. Receivers:
- Logistics is intended to have full access to the number of meals booked by each Company.
- The Duty Officer will have access to the total of the scheduled dismissals, having the possibility to search for the dismissals of a particular Cadet on the online platform. A generic User for the Duty Official should also be created to streamline the service exchange process.
- Duty Cadet will have access to layoffs for his entire Company.
- Schematically, the implementation of the project will make it possible to process the information on dismissals in an accessible way, demonstrated by Figure 7:

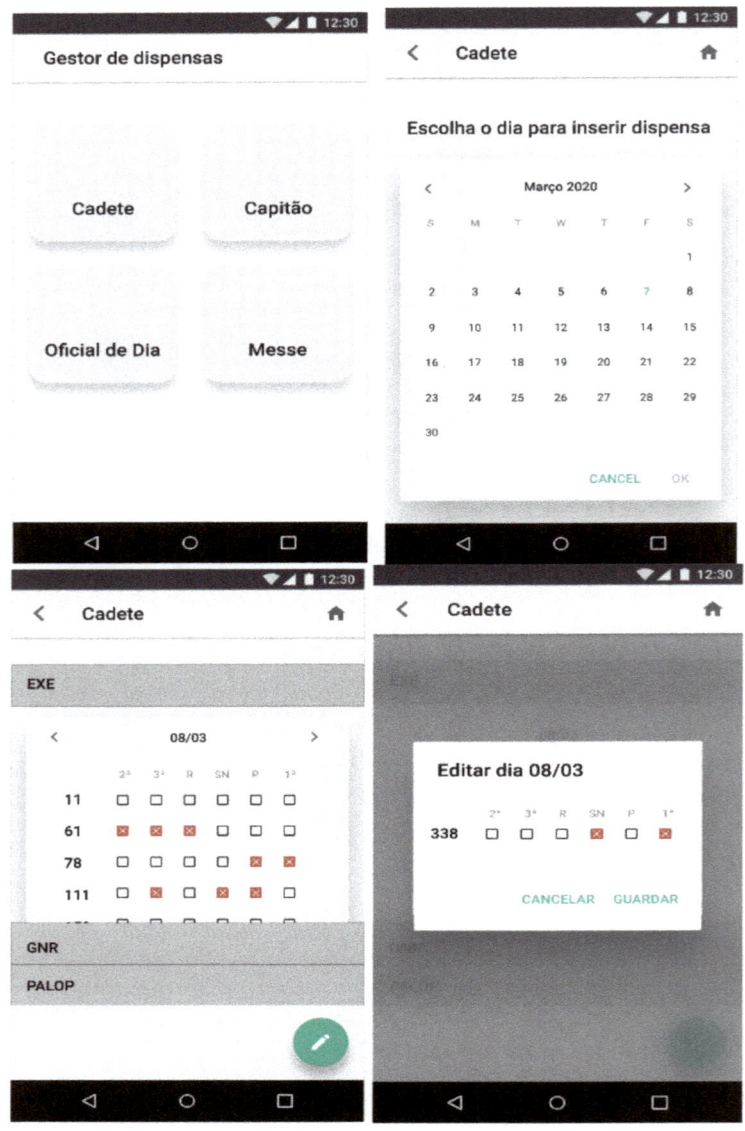

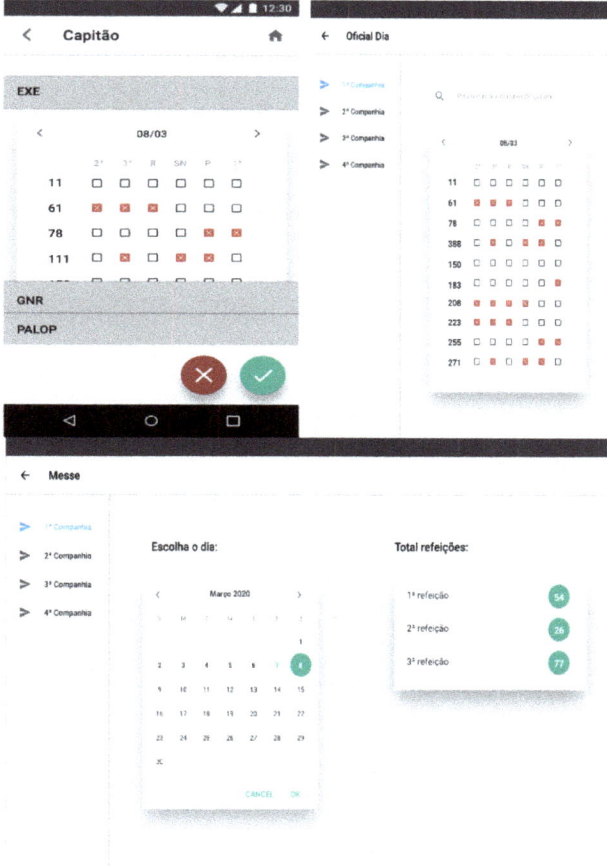

Figure 7: Layout of "Electronic Dispensation Map" project

Tutorial Network Between Cadets

Knowing that the level of demand in higher education is substantially higher than secondary education, this transition, in some cases, can lead to student failure at school. Because of this problem, this project was conceived.

The mentoring network is based on three objectives:

a. Orientation of the academic path of the enrolled students.
b. Early identification of cases of failure.
c. Increase in academic performance.

The Cadet Tutoring Network project is a project that covers all interested Cadets and aims to create a tutoring commission made up of Tutors and Tutors.
a. Tutor:
- Student with evaluation to the Curricular Unit considered by the teaching as extraordinary.
- Previous know of the subject that can help the tutor. Example: Students who have already attended higher education outside the Military Academy.
- A maximum of 5 Cadets per tutor, except in cases of UC with higher failure rates.
- Training in terms of study methods with the support of the Psychopedagogy Support Section.
b. Tutoring:
- Participation in the activities required by the tutor.
- Preparation of final performance report in conjunction with the Psychopedagogy Support Section.

6. Internship in Private Company

As part of the Portuguese State's Central Administration, the Portuguese Army and the GNR are ruled by the International Public Sector Accounting Standards (IPSAS). One of the pillars decreed by the approval of the Portuguese adaptation to IPSAS and which has not yet been fully implemented in the two bodies is Standard No. 27 – Management Accounting. These management reports are still in the embryonic stage in public services. However, the bases of Management/Analytic Accounting are widely disseminated in the demanding standards of management and financial solvency of profit-oriented entities, from which the public entities and the military ones can learn.

This project aims to provide an internship in a private enterprise to the Cadets of the course of Military Administration to obtain an enriching professional experience in applying Management/Analytic Accounting. The basis of the project under implementation contributes to the "triple helix" concept, adding to the excellent performance of the Military Academy in the assessment by stakeholders to improve the training of Military Administration Cadets.

The main goal is that the Cadet, as a future Officer, can contribute with innovations and ways of thinking and solving problems different from those the Army and GNR are familiar with. It is intended to explore beyond the training provided only from the military world, which is the only mean the Cadets have contact with, which does not guarantee evolution, but the continuity of what has been the standard.

7. Plans to further develop the initiative

The integration of Cadets at the end of the course is assured in the Portuguese Army, GNR, or a Portuguese-speaking African countries Army. It was considered mandatory that an investment project's theoretical analysis is not enough as the subject's program. Therefore, the program also included analysing the campus's limitations to develop future skills with application in the military headquarters where the new military Officer will work. The environmental analysis and the ability to surpass the weakness are now academic and socially awarded. This procedure pretends to mitigate the gap between the theoretical analysis of evaluating projects through the experience of conceiving and implementing a project. The alignment of education competencies with the University and campus needs achieve what Samwel Mwasalwiba (2010) reviewed in the literature as something vital: the impact indicators of teaching. The 100% rate of employability after the courses in the Military Academy allows the institution to explore

7.1 European Innovation Council and Small and Medium-sized Enterprises Executive Agency

As a possibility of being part of the jury, institutional collaboration with the Enterprise Europe Network Portugal indicates European internationalisation paths via the European Innovation Council and Small and Medium-sized Enterprises Executive Agency.

Since these are defence-related projects, the logic of the subsequent editions of the Military Shark Tank will be that of "dual-use" usage.

7.2 Portuguese Armed Forces

Another future goal is to replicate the model to the Armed Forces, involving the other military academies: Navy School and Air Force Academy.

The Military Administration speciality formation for officers is similar for the three branches of the Portuguese Armed Forces and the GNR:

- Military Administration | Army
- Naval Administration | Navy

- Aeronautical Administration | Air Force
- Military Administration | GNR (Ministry of Internal Affairs)

Author biography

Major Corguinho Fernandes is a PhD researcher in Economics. He performed technical functions in the financial area. He held leadership roles at Academia Militar, where he is currently a professor. Since 2015, he has performed management functions at the R&D center of Academia Militar.

Bringing NPD into the Virtual Classroom: The WORLDSPORT Simulation

Keith Goffin, Anna Essén, Mattias Nordqvist and Sebastian Krakowski
House of Innovation, Stockholm School of Economics, Sweden
k.goffin@cranfield.ac.uk

Abstract: New product development (NPD) is an important topic in university courses on innovation management. However, the challenges of working in a cross-functional team and bringing a product to market are hard to convey through traditional teaching approaches, such as lectures and case studies. Therefore, an NPD simulation has been developed for teaching BSc and MBA students. Working in teams of six or more, students have to analyse market needs and develop a working mobile phone app within five hours. The WORLDSPORT simulation has now been run successfully six times in an online teaching environment. Overall, it is an engaging way for students to experience NPD under time pressure and it emulates the development and market launch of a real product. It also demonstrates the added challenge that virtual NPD teams currently face, having to coordinate their work online due to the remote working.

Keywords: new product development; innovation teaching; pedagogy; simulations; experiential learning

1. Introduction

New product development (NPD) is a challenging, cross-functional process and one where many companies' new products fail (Cooper & Edgett, 2007; Markham & Lee, 2013). To help prevent product failure, there are many management tools and techniques and, consequently, NPD is an important topic in innovation management courses. However, how can the intensity of NPD be brought into the classroom, so that students experience the challenges for *real*? Answering this question was crucial to the design of a new innovation management course for BSc students. The 'BE701' course was designed and delivered at Stockholm School of Economics (SSE) from January-May 2021 and a central element in this course was an online NPD simulation, where teams of students competed to develop and launch a fully-working product within a few hours. Based on their experiences in the simulation, students are well equipped in subsequent lectures to understand and critically discuss NPD tools and techniques.

Simulations are a powerful tool for management teaching (Heineke & Meile, 1996) and an appropriate pedagogy for undergraduates who have no direct business experience. SSE has used an existing classroom NPD simulation (Goffin & Mitchell, 2006) in MBA teaching for many years and this has proven pedagogical benefits (Cousens, et al, 2009). However, when BE701 was moved online because of Covid-19, a new simulation and an inspiring way to launch the course was needed, and needed within three months.

Based on teaching requirements, the objectives of the initiative were:

1. To develop an online NPD simulation that could be used for 6-hour (maximum) teaching slots in BE701 and various other courses.
2. To enable students to experience the key challenges of NPD:
   - Working in a cross-functional team with associated tensions and communication issues
   - Understanding continuously evolving, ambiguous market requirements
   - Project management under tight timescales
   - Managing project costs, sales and profit
   - Solving technical problems
   - Launching a product in the competitive environment of an industrial fair
   - Using post-project reviews to capture team learning.
3. To make the simulation as realistic as possible.
4. To ensure that the simulation achieves the *Intended Learning Outcomes* (ILOs) within the NPD module of an innovation management course.

It was decided that a viable exercise for students would be to develop a mobile phone app. This requires relatively limited technical expertise and could be based on one of the websites that provide the capability to program and download phone apps. Informal discussions with students confirmed that there was a high level of interest in sports apps and, so, the concept of a 'WORLDSPORT' app that measures a user's fitness was chosen.

To-date, the online simulation has been successfully used in teaching four classes of 75 BSc students and, in addition, two classes of 40 MBAs. As one student commented: *"The WORLDSPORT Simulation was a good learning experience because it* [is]... *like a real business environment within 6 hours. Excellent experience".*

1.1   Overview of the Worldsport simulation

Classes are divided into teams of 6-10 students working together in Zoom breakout rooms. Each team takes the role of a start-up, designing a new app for market launch. Each student chooses one of eight individual roles (CEO, finance, marketing, sports scientist, two software engineers, industrial designer, and project manager). The team must develop an attractive, fully functioning app with an *algorithm* to measure a user's fitness level. With only 5-6 hours available, this is a challenging team task. To understand the simulation from a pedagogical perspective, it helps to consider what takes place before, during, at the end, and after the simulation.

1.2   Before the Simulation

Student teams meet informally in advance, to read their briefing sheets and experiment with app development. The format of the briefing sheets is illustrated by Figures 1, which is for Software Engineer 1 (including a picture of a user interface). The full briefing sheet for the CEO is given in the Appendix.

The briefing sheets for the software engineer give details of how to use the *MIT App Inventor* website, which allows apps to be programmed and loaded onto mobile phones (a Virtual Programming Environment for apps). Figure 2 shows a screenshot from this website with a palette of commands on the left, the user interface in the middle, and further details to the right. The basics of programming are relatively easy to learn and students can access tutorial videos, prepared by a professional app programmer, which explain how to programme algorithms and demonstrate apps.

WORLDSPORT™ PROJECT
Brief for Software Engineer I

Introduction

It is the year 2029 and you work at a small start-up company (currently without a registered name or logo). The company has received [funding to] develop and launch a new sports 'app', aimed at enco[uraging] Europe to actively participate in sports. The idea is [part of the] WORLDSPORT™ initiative to make sports a 'human [right'. The] product development (NPD) team of 6-10 people and n[eeds to be] developing the app, to be launched at ISPO 2030, th[e fair in] Munich. Your app will potentially: allow easy and accur[ate] results; calculate a key fitness measurement; and prov[ide what the] user would most enjoy.

You recently graduated and are now a softwar[e engineer for] new sports 'app' aimed at young people in Europe[. As you have] purchased lots of apps, you have a good idea of the ma[rket. Your tasks] include:

- Setting up the R&D Lab in a separate breakout [room with the other] engineer, the Sports Scientist and the Industrial En[gineer];
- Designing the 'Display Module' for the app, which d[efines how the] app on a smartphone;
- Working together with Software II, programming c[losely and] discussing step-by-step (i.e. block by block);
- Building the complete app with Software Engineer I[I, and the] Sport Empathy Algorithm™ (which calculates a fitn[ess] factor based on physical test results). The algo[rithm will] calculate values that you display on the screen ar[ea and give] and feedback to the user;
- Listening to inputs from marketing;
- Testing and verifying the app's data entry, calculat[ions...];
- Giving estimates of the time you need to the Projec[t Manager];
- Putting your own ideas into the app.

Programming Platform

You and your colleague, Software Engineer II, will be [using the App] Inventor visual programming environment (VPE) http[s://...]. Click the 'Create Apps' button to start programming. You [need to try app] inventor before the simulation starts. A short training [course is] only the software engineers but everyone in your team. [You] and the other software engineer will be programming t[ogether when] running app inventor (this is because combining [two] machines is difficult and will take too much of the t[ime. Two] engineers working together is known as 'extreme prog[ramming'].

¹ See https://www.ispo.com/info/about/purpose

Three video tutorials are available on how the open-source program was coded and other aspects of the App Inventor. These cost €5K each but you think it is well worth the cost, as they will help you to set-up the VPE and code faster. You can watch these in advance but then need to tell the Finance Manager how many you have watched.

The Display Module (Designer Level)

The new sports app needs to have an attractive user interface and to incorporate the complex algorithms. You have heard that young sportspeople prefer yellow as an app background colour easy data entry. The first screen will show your company logo and the client's branding, plus show access to three programs: entering fitness data; calculating training secrets; and calculate sport empathy (what sports the user has an aptitude for). All calculations are based on algorithms that the Sports Scientist has licensed.

The Algorithm Module (Block Level)

This is the responsibility of your colleague, Software Engineer II. Based on big data analysis, which shows that a number of relatively simple fitness tests can be used to calculate a user's overall fitness score and give recommendations about training and

Figure 1: Briefing Sheets for Software Engineer 1.

It should be noted that each briefing sheet gives details of the simulation from one functional perspective and the full picture only emerges if and when a team decides to meet to discuss their roles and develop an overall plan. Furthermore, teams need to consider if they want to buy market research reports to understand the market.

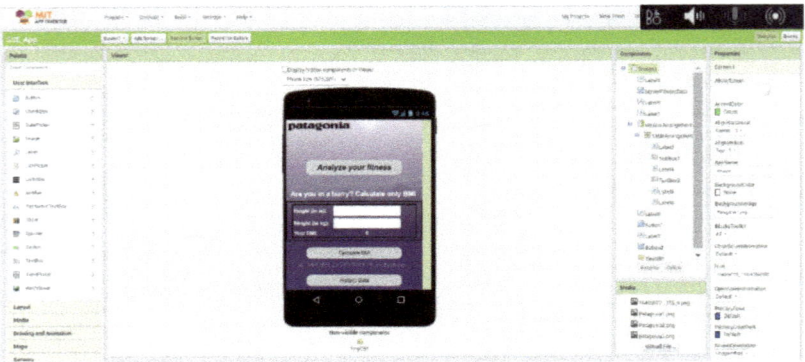

Figure 2: The *MIT App Inventor* Virtual Programming Environment (VPE).

1.3 During the Simulation

The simulation starts with a 15-minute online introduction to the task and Figure 3 shows four of the slides used for this. These cover the session's aims; the challenges teams will face; an explanation of the industrial fair, where the apps will be launched; and a discussion on the algorithm to be implemented.

Figure 3: Example Slides from the Introduction to the Simulation.

Straight after the introduction, students move into their Zoom breakout rooms (two per team; one for management and one for engineers and other technical staff) and start working on their individual tasks. Some teams will arrange regular meetings, others tend to work individually. Whatever approach taken, teams will face significant technical challenges, as the *MIT App Inventor* platform takes time to understand and is quite complicated to demonstrate working apps. To take the edge off the technical challenges, an actual professional app developer is available to provide technical advice to the teams on request.

In addition to technical challenges, teams need to understand user needs, market drivers, and pricing. They can buy market research reports and an example is shown in Figure 4. The market information used in the simulation is based on real figures, extracted from online reports published by real market research agencies, such as Polaris. In addition, every hour teams receive 'CNN News'—i.e. market updates, reflecting the unpredictable flow of information in real NPD situations. Students working in the marketing role must quickly analyse market data and feedback information on key market drivers to their teams.

Some team members have a lot of work whilst others are less pressured and managers that recognize this are allowed to re-assign tasks. However, many teams are so concentrated on their individual roles that they forget to meet regularly. As the teams are working together via Zoom, the problems with communication and coordination of tasks are real and significant, reflecting the current challenges that R&D managers face with Covid-19 remote working. Typically, only half of the teams manage individuals' workloads effectively.

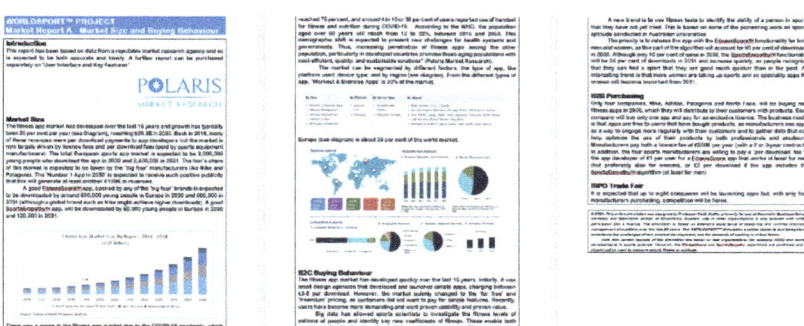

Figure 4: Example Market Report.

Figure 5: Photograph of the Real ISPO Show.

The climax of the simulation is when teams demonstrate their products at a simulated industrial fair. This is based on the real *ISPO* sports industrial fair ('Internationale Fachmesse für Sportartikel und Sportmode', held annually in Munich.) and pictures from this (see Figure 5) and a video are used to set the scene and atmosphere before team presentations commence.

Each team is allowed 3-4 minutes to pitch and demonstrate their app. Figure 6 shows the user interface from a fully-working app developed by a student team. It can be seen that this has been branded to be used with the company Patagonia and it has fields where the user can enter age, resting heart rate, etc. into the app, in order to calculate a fitness score. As each app is demonstrated by a team spokesperson, it is evaluated by faculty using an interactive Excel spreadsheet. (Videos of example student can be viewed on request.) The spreadsheet 'scores' each app, checking whether it has the required product features, which a team should have identified from the information in various market reports. Sales figures and P/L are automatically calculated based on the scoring and, at the end of the presentations, the profit and loss results are announced. The results of the simulation are carefully balanced so that, typically, 30% of teams do not launch a product that is successful on the market (mirroring the research of

Castellion & Markham, 2013); 35% make some profit; and 35% achieve substantial profits.

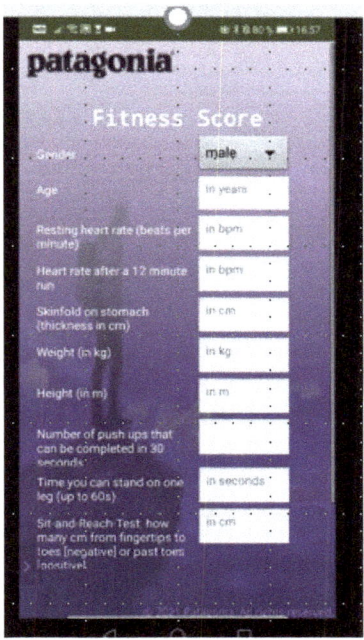

Figure 6: User Interface of a Student Team's App.

End of the Simulation

The simulation finishes with the spreadsheet results being published and teams being told whether they achieved a profit or a loss. Teams are then given 20 minutes to conduct a *post-project review* (Koners & Goffin, 2007), in which they must identify three things 'to improve' and 'how' and complete a standard form. For example, one student team identified their *time management*, *communication*, and *attention to KPIs* (key performance indicators) as their key learning (see Figure 7).

After the Simulation

In the simulation, students have experienced many of the issues that real NPD teams face, such as dispersed collaboration and changing market requirements. This means that their 'lessons learnt' are directly relevant to and can be included in subsequent lectures. Across the different teams, the post-project reviews are aggregated are included in a subsequent lecture on NPD tools and techniques (Figure 8). This provides a rich set of examples of where the students think product development teams can improve and can be incorporated into discussions around management tools and techniques for NPD.

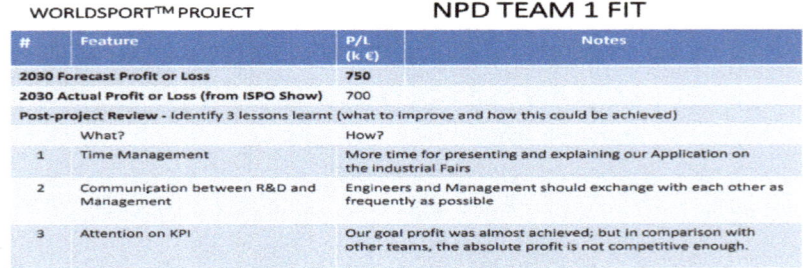

Figure 7: Example Post-project Review Summary Form (Team1 'Fit').

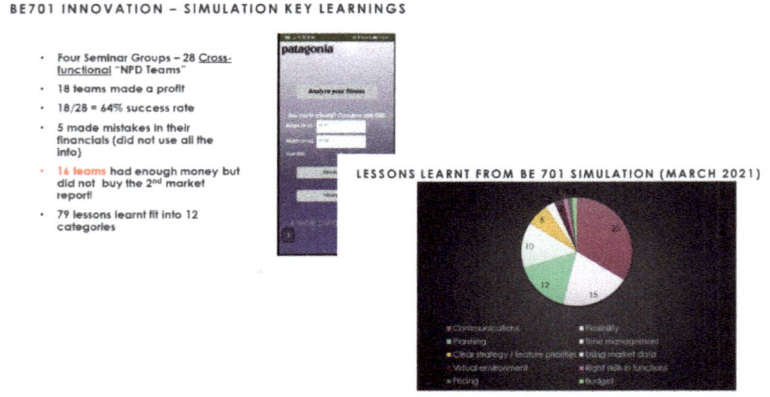

Figure 8: Example Slides from the Subsequent Lecture on NPD.

2. Simulation Infrastructure

Now the simulation has been run six times, the infrastructure is robust. It consists of:

1) Easy-to-understand documentation consisting of briefing sheets; introductory slides; video tutorials; app evaluation spreadsheet, etc.
2) Two faculty members (or one and a teaching assistant) to supervise the simulation. Both must have read all of the briefing sheets, to be able to answer teams' questions about the business challenge. A detailed set of timings for teachers is also available.
3) Student teams require laptops and to download some software in advance.
4) Class size can be from 40 to 75 students, divided into 6-7 teams.
5) The host institution needs a Zoom licence that can accommodate the number of participating students and allow sufficient breakout rooms. For 7 teams, a total of 15 breakout rooms are required (two per team and one extra). Breakout rooms must be pre-configured for easy access and so that students can share screens and data easily.
6) Video tutorials for students on the technical aspects. In addition, a professional app programmer is available to answer students' questions during 2-3 hours of the simulation. This has added further realism and students are impressed at being able to talk to a professional.

3. The Challenges

Designing, testing and launching a teaching simulation within three months was demanding and involved eight main challenges:

1) The first challenge was to identify a task that students can conduct within a few hours, online. The idea of an app emerged when the faculty team considered products that today's students use regularly.
2) The need was for a virtual programming environment that could be quickly understood but was sophisticated enough to enable a complex programming task. Internet searches identified possibilities such as *Altova, Google Play* and *MIT App Inventor*. At this stage, a professional app developer was engaged to support the development of the simulation. Having reviewed several platforms, he recommended *MIT App Inventor*. It allows mobile phone apps with attractive user interfaces and sophisticated algorithms to be developed.
3) The business aspects of the simulation were crucial, included defining the task. Student teams must develop an app to take users' manually entered values (including their height, weight and heart rate) and calculate a 'fitness score'. The main challenge in developing the business aspects of the simulation was writing simple, concise briefing

sheets for the different roles (including the CEO, finance director, software engineers, etc.). In writing the briefing sheets, the complete information about the task was deliberately distributed across the various roles with some planned overlaps. This meant that each individual only had access to portions of the full information——making it necessary for team members to communicate effectively with each other.
4) The technical aspects of developing an app to calculate fitness score was conducted in cooperation with the professional app developer. One faculty member also learnt to use App Inventor, so that a working app (including a sophisticated algorithm) could be prepared. Based on this experience, the briefing sheets for the technical roles (including software and the sports scientist) were improved and video tutorials were recorded.
5) To ensure that the simulation was viable within the 5-6 hour teaching slot available, a pilot run was conducted with the BE701 faculty team and teaching assistants. With some help from the professional programmer, this group of seven people was able to program a partly-working app within three hours, demonstrating the simulation's viability.
6) An important aspect was to make the simulation as realistic as possible and four steps were taken to achieve this. First, the real market for sports apps was researched and key elements were incorporated; including details of the ISPO industrial fair; information from real market reports; and real pricing. Second, the fitness score algorithm is contrived but it adopts some aspects from sports science, such as Body Mass Index (BMI) and maximum recommended heart rate during training. Third, the professional programmer's availability to give advice during the teaching sessions adds an extra element of realism and generally encouraged teams to achieve more than what they thought was possible at the beginning of the simulation. Fourth, the challenges included in the NPD simulation were based on typical problems that NPD teams face, as determined from a range of research papers (Balachandra & Friar, 1997; Castellion & Markham, 2013; Cooper, 1998; Cooper & Kleinschmidt, 2007; Harvard Business School, 2013; Markham &, 2013;).
7) It was necessary to make the simulation robust enough that it could be supervised by different faculty in three parallel sessions (to fit the SSE BE701 timetable). This meant that the introduction to the simulation

was recorded in advance, timings were set carefully (and followed), and one faculty member was available to provide extra support across the three parallel sessions.
8) It is important to verify that the simulation is an effective teaching mechanism. The simulation gives students the opportunity to experience the typical problems encountered in NPD, so that they can better understand why management tools and techniques are required and how these approaches work. Given this background, valid and reliable ways of evaluating the simulation are needed.

4. How the initiative was received

The simulation is still new and has only been used six times. Consequently, the amount of specific, quantitative feedback that has been gathered to-date is limited. However, student qualitative feedback has been collated and, for the coming year, more formal ways of measuring how well the ILOs have been met are being developed.

BE701 Feedback (SSE)

We received numerous comments from the four groups of 75 SSE students during and after the simulation. They expressed their appreciation of the hands-on experience which gave them insights into NPD. One representative comment was: *"During the course we did the fitness score app contest. That was a very interesting exercise that I liked and I really think it should be kept in the course"*. Others appreciated the novel, dramatic start to the BE701 course (the simulation was deliberately chosen for the opening sessions of the BE701 course [four separate groups of 75 students]). Although some students expected the simulation to be exhausting, many said they found it fun and exciting, especially the ISPO fair at the end of the exercise.

In addition to general comments, the results of the BE701 teams' post-project reviews are an important pointer to the learning enabled by the simulation. Across the 28 teams, the 79 separate learning points were collated and sorted into 12 categories (see Figure 8). The most frequently mentioned ones were: *Communications* (between different members of the team and, particularly, between the management and engineering factions), *flexibility* (in responding to changing market needs); *project planning* (deciding what could be achieved) and; *time management* (ensuring that the product was ready for the ISPO Show). It will be shown that these categories closely reflect the ILOs for the simulation, which will be discussed below.

The experience in SSE showed that the simulation could be used with 6-7 teams and up to 75 students. However, the MIT App Inventor website tools for demonstrating apps were found difficult to use and time-consuming for teams to learn. This led to tips about potential technical difficulties being added to the briefing sheets and the decision was made to always have the professional app programmer available, in order to help teams know how they could best demonstrate their apps.

MBA Feedback (Mannheim Business School)

Approximately three months after the BE701 teaching in Stockholm, two separate online Executive MBA classes of 40 students were held online for Mannheim Business School. Although EMBA students have much more business experience than BSc students, many of them have not worked directly on NPD projects themselves and so the simulation is still very relevant for them. MBS students were encouraged to adopt a role outside their previous experience with, for example, R&D people taking a marketing role and vice-versa.

In preparation for the EMBA sessions, the technical aspects of the simulation were further embellished (in particular, the way to demonstrate apps) and, in addition, a questionnaire was designed to establish if the ILOs were being achieved. This questionnaire was piloted in July 2021 and selected results are shown in Table 1. Another aspect of the MBA teaching is that the course assignment has been partly linked to the simulation. MBA teams must produce a 4-minute video summarizing what they learnt in a way that would help other teams be more effective in managing NPD. These assignments will be submitted in late August 2021 and their value be evaluated then.

5. Learning outcomes and further development

Over the six times the simulation has been run in SSE and Mannheim, students have found it a challenging exercise and only 60% of teams have successfully created an app and made a profit. Table 1 shows the three ILOs for the simulation, compared to students' learning (as indicated by BE701 post-project reviews and MBA qualitative feedback). Importantly, it appears that the learning and ILOs are very closely aligned.

Table 1: Intended Learning Outcomes.

#	At the end of this session students have...	Explanation	Examples of how this is achieved in the simulation	Comments based on student feedback (BE701 post-project reviews or MBA qualitative feedback)
1	Experienced the challenges involved in managing cross-functional teams.	Working in a cross-functional team with associated tensions and communication issues	No single briefing sheet explains everything about the simulation / Briefing sheets include different functional goals that are conflicting / Management and engineering teams are in separate Zoom rooms.	Communication issues clearly emerged in the results (BE701) / "Taking a specific role... puts yourself in the shoes of others... Very nice way of learning" (MBA)
		Understanding continuously evolving, ambiguous market requirements	The market reports must be carefully analysed to eliminate ambiguity / Market requirements evolve during the simulation via CNN News.	Flexibility to deal with evolving markets clearly emerged (BE701) / "Understand customer needs, screen the internal ideas, and convert them into product" (MBA).
		Project management under tight timescales	Teams need to be very efficient to complete a working product / The time is typically too short for 30% of the teams.	Time management issues clearly emerged (BE701 / "It showed in real time how innovation can happen and how fast it can go". (MBA).
		Managing project costs, sales and profit	Profit can only be achieved with a working app with many of the required features / Only apps with <u>every</u> required feature will make high profits.	"The other teams' inspired me to think in different ways" (MBA); "Follow disciplined process and always pay attention on P&L" (MBA).

#	At the end of this session students have...	Explanation	Examples of how this is achieved in the simulation	Comments based on student feedback (BE701 post-project reviews or MBA qualitative feedback)
		Solving technical problems	The *MIT App Inventor* platform is not so easy to learn and demonstrating apps is slow and, somewhat, unreliable / Programming the app requires constant testing and problem-solving.	*"30 minutes before the presentation, my formula [algorithm] was wrong but I could correct it... we got the best score!"* (MBA).
		Launching a product in the competitive environment of an industrial fair	The short time available puts pressure on the teams /This culminates in the ISPO Show, where presenters know they 'need to perform'.	*"We need to create value for customers or end-users, find customers' hidden needs, develop unique, differentiated app"* (MBA). *"Understand the customer need is the most important part"* (MBA).
2	Analysed the key issues involved in managing NPD.	Using post-project reviews to capture team learning.	The post-project reviews focus teams on three key leaning points (*what* to improve and *how*) / Post-session reading (Goffin et al, 2010) reinforces the importance of post-project reviews.	*It gave me a better understanding of the difficulty of innovation"* (MBA).
3	The experience to better understand tools and	Experience of and reflection on the simulation forms the foundation to	The whole class has shared experience of the simulation which provides concrete	*"It simulates the actual working scenario... experience* [on] *how to deal with the*

#	At the end of this session students have...	Explanation	Examples of how this is achieved in the simulation	Comments based on student feedback (BE701 post-project reviews or MBA qualitative feedback)
	techniques for NPD (in subsequent lectures).	understand abstract concepts (c.f. Kolb & Fry, 1975).	examples that can be incorporated into the classroom discussions / Across the class, all of the typical problems with NPD have been experienced and understood.	*similar work in my real working life* (MBA); *"In order to coordinate better the project schedule and product development,* [and] *marketing approach"* (MBA).

The simulation will now be used regularly in teaching NPD at SSE and Mannheim. Further, deeper assessment is ongoing and, for example, a statistical analysis of students' learning will be applied to the simulation in the near future. In addition, learning theory will be applied to further strengthen the simulation's pedagogy. The well-known experiential learning cycle (Kolb & Fry, 1975) stresses the importance of: 1) Concrete experience; 2) Observation of and reflection on that experience; 3) Formation of abstract concepts based upon the reflection and; 4) Testing the new concepts. The first two of these are attained through the simulation itself and the post-project review respectively, whereas the third is covered in the subsequent lectures on NPD tools and techniques. The faculty team is now considering how the fourth step of the experiential learning, cycle testing new concepts, can be integrated into the pedagogy of the simulation. Thus, the simulation can still be viewed as 'work-in-progress'.

References

Balachandra, R. & Friar, J.H. (1997) Factors for Success in R&D Projects and New Product Development. *IEEE Transactions on Engineering Management*, 44 (3), 276–87.

Castellion, G. & Markham, S.K. (2013) Perspective: New Product Failure Rates: Influence of Argumentum ad Populum and Self-Interest. *Journal of Product Innovation Management*, 30 (5), 976-979.

Cooper, R.G. (1998) *Product leadership: Creating and Launching Superior New Products*. Reading, MASS, Perseus Books.

Cooper, R.G. & Edgett, S.J. (2007) *Generating Breakthrough New Product Ideas: Feeding the Innovation Funnel*. Ancaster, Canada, Product Development Institute.

Cooper, R.G. & Kleinschmidt, E.J. (2007) Winning Businesses in Product Development: The Critical Success Factors. *Research-Technology Management*, 50 (3), 52–65.

Cousens, A., Goffin, K., Mitchell, R., Van der Hoven, C. & Szwejczewski, M. (2009) Teaching New Product Development Using the 'CityCar' Simulation". *Creativity and Innovation Management*, 18 (3), 176-189.

Goffin, K., Koners, U., Baxter, D. & Van Der Hoven, C. (2010) Managing Tacit Knowledge and Lessons Learned in New Product Development. *Research Technology Management*, 53 (4), 39-51.

Goffin, K. & Mitchell, R. (2006) Teaching New Product Development Using the 'Cranfield CityCar' Simulation. *BizEd*, V (2), 42-45.

Harvard Business School (2013) *On Innovation*. Boston, US, Harvard Business School Publishing.

Heineke, J.N. & Meile, L.C. (1995) *Games and Exercises for Operations Management: Hands-on Learning Activities for Basic Concepts and Tools*. Englewood Cliffs, NJ, Prentice-Hall International.

Kolb, D. A. & Fry, R.E. (1975) Towards an applied theory of experiential learning. In Cooper, Cary L. (ed.). *Theories of group processes*. London, New York, Wiley, 33–58.

Koners, U. & Goffin, K. (2007) Learning from Post-Project Reviews: A Cross-Case Analysis. *Journal of Product Innovation Management*, 24 (3), 242-258.

Markham, S.K. & Lee, H. (2013) Product Development and Management Association's 2012 Comparative Performance Assessment Study. *Journal of Product Innovation Management*, 30 (3), 408-429

APPENDIX: CEO Briefing Sheet

WORLDSPORT™ PROJECT
Brief for CEO

Introduction

It is the year 2029 and you work at a small start-up company (currently without a registered name or logo). The company has received significant venture capital to develop and launch a new sports 'app', aimed at encouraging more young people in Europe to actively participate in sports. The idea is related to the sport industry's WORLDSPORT™ initiative to make sports a 'human right'[1]. You are part of a new product development (NPD) team of 6-10 people and need to meet a tight schedule in developing the app, to be launched at ISPO 2030, the annual industry exhibition in Munich. Your app will: allow easy and accurate entry of a user's fitness test results; calculate a key fitness measurement; and provide advice on which sports the user would most enjoy.

As CEO you need to meet a tight schedule in designing and launching a new app onto the market. Your key responsibilities include:

- Chairing a meeting with the team to launch the project;
- Making strategic decisions as required;
- Approving the financial decisions with a budget of €400K;
- Co-ordinating the team's efforts through the project manager;
- Ensuring that the team's resources are used effectively. You are allowed to reassign tasks across the team members, if you wish;
- Monitoring the project schedule;
- Making the final choice on who will present the app at ISPO and ensuring that they arrive on-time at the 'ISPO Presenters' Room';
- At the end of the project, ensuring that your team conducts an effective post-project review and report P/L and three key lessons learnt.

The Company Team

You have used your business skills to convince venture capitalists to fund the start-up and have recruited a team with the right skills and experience. Currently, the team of 6-10 people consists of:

- Yourself, the CEO.
- 1-2 Finance Managers (with degrees in accountancy and extensive controlling experience in various companies).
- Two Software Engineers (for coding the app user interface and the algorithm for calculating fitness levels and aptitude for different sports).
- A Sports Scientist (who is an expert in fitness testing and professional and amateur training regimes) and could be a good presenter of your app;
- A Project Manager (with experience of managing projects in the automotive industry). [In small teams the CEO will also take this role.]
- 1-2 Marketing Managers (one focused on user needs / usability and the other more experienced in market size projections).
- An Industrial Designer (who is expert in the impact of aesthetics and web design) and could also be a good presenter.

---
[1] See https://www.ispo.com/en/about/purpose

[In teams of 6: there will only be one marketing person; one finance manager; the CEO will also be responsible for project management; and the sports scientist will need to cover industrial design issues. <u>Whatever your actual team size, your finance manager will need to budget for 10 people in your financial planning.</u>]

The ISPO Trade Fair

ISPO is a yearly trade fair show where all of the major manufacturers of sport articles exhibit their innovations and discuss how sport can be promoted worldwide. This is an important event, the culmination of your team's work, and the only chance for you to sell your 'product' (your app) to manufacturers. This where your team has to convince managers from various international companies that your app is the best one for their customers. The quality of your sales presentation and app demonstration at the show is vital. You are advised to prepare it carefully and to make an effective demonstration, as you and competitors are allocated <u>only 3 minutes each</u> (this will be strictly controlled). This is your only opportunity to generate sales in 2030. ISPO will be covered live by a leading television channel.

At ISPO, only one member of the team may give the sales presentation and demonstrate the app, unaided by others. The rest of the team will have other tasks to do and you do not have the funds for everyone to travel to Munich. The doors of the exhibition hall will open to admit your presenter to the 'Presenters' Room' at an allotted time. A reminder signal will be given 5 minutes beforehand. If your presenter is late, they will be refused entry. **Note: Venture capitalists expect to see profit on sales made at the ISPO trade fair. They will withdraw their support from any company that does make a profit in 2030!**

© 2021. This online simulation was designed by Professor Keith Goffin, primarily for use at Mannheim Business School, Germany and Stockholm School of Economics, Sweden. Use in other organizations is only allowed with written permission and a licence. The simulation is based on extensive experience of designing and running innovation management simulations over the last 20 years. The WORLDSPORT™ Simulation enables students and delegates to experience the challenges of new product development, and the demands of working in virtual teams.

Note that certain aspects of the simulation are based on real organizations (for example ISPO) and current developments in sports science. However, the FitnessScore and SportsEmpathy algorithms are contrived and so should not be used to measure sports fitness or aptitude.

Author Biographies

Keith Goffin is a Research Professor at Stockholm School of Economics and Emeritus Professor at Cranfield School of Management, UK. Before joining academia, he worked in the medical electronics industry. He has published widely and his research focuses on achieving growth through innovation and generating deep customer insights.

Anna Essén's research concerns emergent and organized innovation aiming for complex solutions and involving public and private actors. Current projects concern cross-sectoral innovation collaborations in relation to autonomous transport markets and smart cities, and the design of ecosystems aiming for prevention innovation. She publishes in journals such as Human Relations, and Organization Studies.

Mattias Nordqvist is Professor in Business Administration with a focus on Entrepreneurship at the House of Innovation (HOI), Stockholm School of Economics (SSE). His teaching, research and outreach activities concentrate on entrepreneurship, strategic renewal and governance in closely held, private companies, in particular, family businesses. He focuses on both start-ups/new ventures and established companies.

Sebastian Krakowski is an Assistant Professor at the Stockholm School of Economics and has an educational background in economics and management. He obtained his Ph.D. at the University of Geneva and was previously a visiting researcher at Warwick Business School. His research interests include artificial intelligence, behavioral theory, and strategy

Fostering Innovation and Entrepreneurship Skills in Tourism and Hospitality Higher Education: The Case of the Event Management Learning Model

Susana Filipa Gonçalves, Ana Gonçalves, Elsa Correia Gavinho, Francisco Silva, Victor Alves Afonso and Cláudia Lopes
Estoril Higher Institute for Tourism and Hotel Studies, Portugal

susana.goncalves@eshte.pt; ana.goncalves@eshte.pt; elsa.gavinho2@eshte.pt; francisco.silva@eshte.pt; victor.afonso@eshte.pt; claudia.r.lopes@eshte.pt

1. Introduction

The *Event Management Learning Model* (EMLM) is a practical project that brings together different curricular units in the 3rd year of the undergraduate degree in Leisure Management and Tourism Entertainment at the Estoril Higher Institute for Tourism and Hotel Studies (ESHTE) in Portugal. This learning model invites teams of 4 to 6 students to develop the concept, plan, implement, and evaluate real-life events under lecturers' guidance, coaching and incentive. Lecturers become 'learning facilitators' instead of 'classic' higher education lecturers. The EMLM has been evolving since 2007 and has been implemented in its current format since 2016/2017 with the following objectives:

1. to give students a central role in their learning process by letting them choose the project they want to develop according to the contents addressed in each of the curricular units involved.

2. to promote an environment that allows students to acquire innovation and entrepreneurship skills and to adapt to ever-changing realities, which are mandatory skills in the events business.

3. to enable students to gain autonomy, not only by adapting theory to real-context situations but also in the decision-making process

entailed in planning and implementing events, thus promoting the development of students' transversal skills.

The EMLM consists of 5 stages, applied in 2 semesters over an academic year:

i. **Idea Camp** – This 5-hour workshop borrows on some of the methodologies used in the Disney Creativity Strategy developed by Dilts (1994) and in the 2015 European Cultural Foundation Idea Camp. Creativity is the focal point: students are asked to bring materials and to prepare the visual identification of the team; the room layout allows each team to sit on chairs or to use the floor as they please; inspiring music and posters help stimulating a creative ambience and mood. However, to support students achieve the ideation goal of deciding the event that they are going to produce, tasks are time-limited. Student teams are initially invited to note down as many ideas as possible for the event concept. These ideas are then assessed by the other teams according to specific criteria defined by students; this is done on a rolling basis until only one idea is left. Each team is then asked to detail one of the ideas by filling in a large poster with pre-given topics. The final task consists of displaying the posters on which students and lecturers provide feedback and suggestions for improvement through post-its and conversation.

Figure 1: Examples of the 2018 and 2020 Idea Camps

ii. **Project Camp** – About a month after the Idea Camp, teams deliver a 10-minute pitch and receive feedback and questions from *alumni*, now employed in events businesses, invited lecturers, and trade specialists from the public, private and third sectors, working in areas related to the projects developed. The mood in this phase is more formal to bring teams to a professional context. This stage acts as an exceptional opportunity to gather additional comments on the project from experienced professionals and establish partnerships with the guests' companies or entities.

Figure 2: Example of the 2019 Project Camp

iii. **Event planning** – An event plan is delivered by each team at the end of the 1st semester, which contains general information about the event, its strategic, tactical, and production planning, and specific aspects required under each curricular unit. Its delivery takes place about three weeks after the Project Camp, and students can improve their work following the input provided by experts. However, during the 2nd semester, this plan will need to be improved and adapted to the reality of contacts and confirmations that each team establishes. During this period, student teams are supported by lecturers in tutorial meetings throughout the semester, some of them mandatory, and others by request depending on the needs of each project. These moments are crucial to guide students through their decision-making process and require an intensive engagement and commitment from teachers, who also keep up with the process by email and via WhatsApp with each team. The practical classes in which teams structure some parts of the plan, such as the promotional plan, the logistics plan, the budget, or the evaluation plan, are also relevant to guide the learning process, especially to help students on how to adapt theory to practice. Final updated strategic and tactical plans are delivered one month before the event implementation, and the production plan and monitoring documents for production one week before, especially because some teams might have decided to make substantial changes to the event plan delivered in the previous semester. Another important moment during this process is the 50-minute pitch presented in class since this promotes the discussion about the solutions to the different constraints and challenges that each team encounters, promoting collaboration work between all the teams, some of which (have) encounter(ed) similar difficulties.

iv. **Production** – The event pre-production phase includes all preparation tasks entirely performed by students: the contact with all the stakeholders involved (public and private entities, suppliers, sponsors and partners, volunteers, media, among others), site inspections to venues, contracts, licensing, and promotion. The event's actual implementation takes place in the 2nd semester, and is done under the lecturers' guidance and supervision, including assembly/staging, briefings, the event itself, disassembly, and debriefings. In the pandemic context the need to find new solutions to stage events (e.g., digital, hybrid or streaming) allowed students and teachers to develop their innovation skills to adapt to a whole new reality that, at the same time, events management companies were facing.

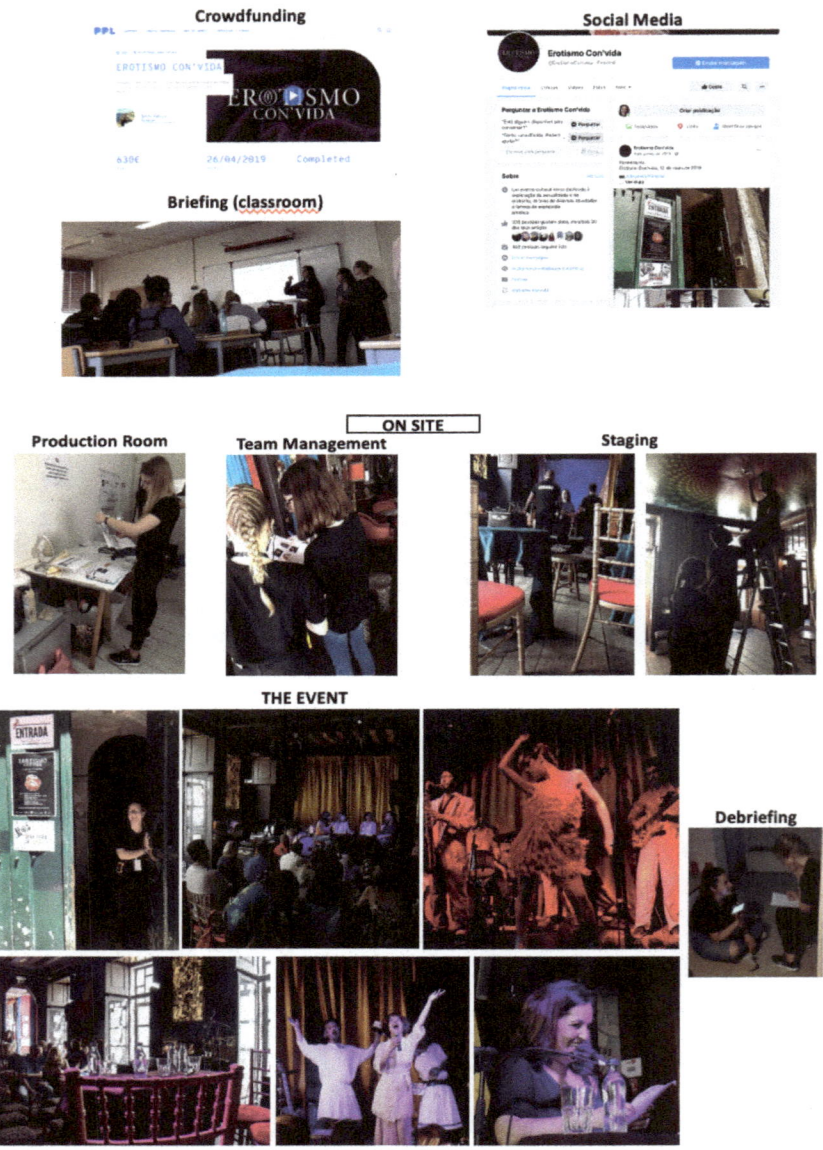

Figure 3: Example of an event production in 2018/2019

v. **Evaluation** – Events are evaluated by students, in a final report, based on the data collected during the whole process. This includes the team's internal evaluation, but also external data from participants, suppliers, partners, sponsors, public, private and/or third sector entities, external evaluators, and staff. An individual student report is also produced with personal reflections related to: self-assessment; assessment of the team performance concerning the different processes, time management, delivery capacity, relationships, and leadership; assessment of the performance of each team member; and the event evaluation. This takes place as if students are external evaluators, by considering only the staff briefing, the event production, and debriefings. 30-minute individual discussions about the whole learning process with the lecturer who has supervised the event are also conducted and are essential to assess the involvement of each student in the management process, their learning path and achievements, and to fully understand the team's organisation and decision-making processes.

2. The infrastructure

This innovative and structured hands-on teaching-learning initiative brings together six lecturers from five different curricular units from cross-cutting areas such as cultural management, events management, tourism entertainment, and marketing. These lecturers have different academic backgrounds that range from undergraduate to post-doc degrees in the areas of expertise mentioned above and are also entrepreneurs and practitioners in events management, most of them for more than 20 years. This interdisciplinary, intergenerational, gender-balanced, and nonhierarchical learning facilitation team is the backbone of the EMLM. A friendly and collaborative working environment composed of people who share the same pedagogical vision and objectives is key to the success of this initiative.

This teaching team hosts regular meetings to agree on the guidelines for the development of the different stages of the process, to prepare and coordinate their implementation, and to collect assessment data tools (e.g. student surveys, interviews with Project Camp guests, and meetings with student teams). A Moodle platform page, shared and managed by all lecturers and made available to students, is crucial in providing all the necessary information about the various learning moments and for students to deliver their assignments throughout the process.

The active participation of *alumni*, other ESHTE lecturers and experts from events businesses in the Project Camp is also pivotal to ensure that student teams receive realistic feedback and valuable suggestions that help them improve their event concepts and future implementation.

In addition, a supportive institutional environment where entrepreneurial initiatives across disciplines and scientific and administrative departments are welcomed is essential to accomplish the different stages and goals defined under the EMLM. For the Idea Camp and the Project Camp, as well as for the production stage collaboration with ESHTE's presidency, the undergraduate degree's coordination, the communication and events department, and the IT department is vital since the implementation of these stages requires specific permissions as well as facilities with suitable sound, IT and visual projection equipment, even though there is no institutional funding allocated to these projects.

3. Challenges

1. Several challenges have been encountered throughout the development of this innovative and entrepreneurial teaching-learning initiative and have called for specific actions. These include:

    i. The alignment of syllabi, namely the theoretical component of each curricular unit involved, since the goal is that all curricular units complement each other and simultaneously contribute to improving the development of students' work. Therefore, a preparation meeting with all the lecturers who participate in this project is held at the beginning of each academic year to plan the themes to be addressed and the guidelines to be presented to students in the first week of classes.

    ii. The initial definition of assessment indicators that reflect the work carried out by student teams and their performance throughout the process; these indicators seek to reduce subjectivity and variation in lecturers' assessment methods.

    iii. Time-consuming tasks, both for lecturers and student teams, which requires an adequate integration of several curricular units to make the work undertaken by teams more fruitful.

iv. The economic and social environment, which students analyse and within which the project is developed, influencing many of the decisions made. This renowned learning method allows for a better understanding of how the context in which students are integrated can influence their work. The current pandemic situation, which has affected the 2019/2020 and 2020/2021 academic years by moving classes to a context of emergency remote teaching-learning, has intensified the need to interpret an increasingly uncertain environment, to design projects accordingly, and to define adequate strategies that would still enable the development of a practical component of students' learning.

v. The constant update regarding the digital tools used, considering market needs and the increasing digitisation of contemporary societies, demands continuous learning from lecturers and students who, in many cases, undertake a shared learning path of digital literacy.

vi. The ideation process and the possibility for students to freely choose event themes, as well as the type of events to be implemented, call for a constant revision of legal issues in place and the detailed monitoring of each project's needs.

Additionally, teams' different rhythms and the need for lecturers' adaptation concerning project monitoring (namely through tutorial meetings and constant communication by e-mail or via WhatsApp, as mentioned earlier), as well as the possibility to learn from mistakes, must be highlighted as crucial elements for students' reflection and potential improvement, either as a team, with lecturers and colleagues, or even individually. The EMLM is, therefore, driven by a holistic and transdisciplinary teaching-learning approach that allows for a more comprehensive and cohesive approach to the various curricular units but also for a solid connection to the labour market.

4. How the initiative is received

The participants involved in the project can be divided into three groups: i) students; ii) lecturers from the curricular units involved in the initiative; and iii) experts invited to the panel of specialists who provide feedback on students' projects at the Project Camp. Concerning the reception of the initiative from this last group, this may be demonstrated by the feedback they provide at the Project Camp, together with data collected from the interviews undertaken with them after they participate in this stage. Moreover, the collaboration of various entities and market players in supporting the implementation of events in a real-life context must also be emphasised as they are crucial for the idea of the event to become a reality.

Lecturers, on the other hand, have shown significant involvement in the project, motivated by the possibility of collaborative work which facilitates better articulation between the different curricular contents and thus the possibility to obtain better results.

As for learners' reception of the initiative, in addition to the more informal approaches resulting from participant observation throughout the entire learning process, which also includes image and video recording, questionnaires are applied to students in 3 (three) different moments: 2 (two) in the 1st semester, one after the Idea Camp and the other after the Project Camp, in order to understand their perception about each of these stages, and later, in the 2nd semester, after the events' production. A synthesis of these results is shown in Tables 1 and 2.

Table 1. Project Camp (PC) and Idea Camp (IC) reception (2018/2019, 2019/2020 and 2020/2021)

Statements	Stage	Frequency (%) Likert scale - 1 (totally disagree) to 5 (totally agree)					Total of responses	Average	Mode	Median
		1	2	3	4	5				
The model allows a better understanding of the application of theoretical contents taught in class	PC	0.7	6.3	28.7	44.8	19.6	143	3.76	4	4
	IC	0.0	6.5	29.9	46.8	16.9	154	3.74	4	4
With this model, I feel more motivated to study these curricular units	PC	0.7	4.9	31.3	38.9	24.3	144	3.81	4	4
	IC	0.0	3.2	18.8	36.4	41.6	154	4.16	5	4
The project makes all the difference to the work we are carrying out as a team	PC	2.1	2.1	14.6	32.6	48.6	144	4.24	5	4
	IC	0.7	4.6	13.1	35.9	45.8	153	4.22	5	4

The analysis of these results shows that the EMLM is highly valued by students; indeed, about 82% consider that the project makes all the difference for enhanced teamwork. 64.1% also consider that this model allows for a better understanding of the application of theoretical content, and 70.6% feel more motivated to study. These results are reinforced by the data provided on the questionnaire applied after the event production, with 95.9% of students reporting that the development of the project has a high (17.8%) or very high (78.1%) importance for their learning process (Table 2).

Table 2. Planning and Management in Tourism Entertainment curricular unit – Importance of the development of the project for the learning process (2018/2019 and 2019/2020)

	Frequency - Likert scale: 1 (very low) to 5 (very high)					Total of responses	Average	Mode	Median
	1	2	3	4	5				
n	0	1	2	13	57	73	4.7	5	5
%	0.0	1.4	2.7	17.8	78.1	100.0			

5. Learning outcomes

Learning outcomes are assessed through: i) project follow-up meetings; ii) questionnaires applied to students at 3 (three) crucial learning stages (after the Idea Camp, after the Project Camp and after the event's implementation); iii) success rate in project implementation; iv) students' records/comments in the final stage of the process; and v) students' approval rate in the curricular units involved. The follow-up meetings, both individual and as a team, are an exceptional opportunity to assess the development of the learning process and the work carried out by each student team and individual team member. From the analysis of the questionnaires, the value assigned to the curricular unit in which the events are implemented stands out, with 90.6% of students considering that the contribution of this curricular unit to their learning process is either high (37.3%) or very high (53.3% (Table 3).

Table 3. Contribution of the curricular unit in which events are produced to students' learning process (2018/2019 and 2019/2020)

	Frequency - Likert scale: from 1 – very low to 5 very high					Total of responses	Average	Mode	Median
	1	2	3	4	5				
n	0	0	7	28	40	75	4.44	5	5
%	0.0	0.0	9.3	37.3	53.3	100.0			

It should also be noted that the Idea Camp and the Project Camp are essential moments for the development and consolidation of ideas in the process of creating and designing the event. The contribution of the Project Camp stands out, with most students reporting that they will consider the criticisms/suggestions made by experts and will analyse how these can contribute to improving their project (Table 4). Thus, the fact that the Project Camp has a panel of renowned experts is highly valued; it gives students a sense of reality as they realise that their ideas can indeed be brought to life and establishes a closer connection to the market as they understand how the market reacts to their idea.

Table 4. "Please mention what best characterises the contribution of the Project Camp for the team project" (2019-20 and 2020-21)

Contribution of the Project Camp for the team project	IC	PC
Before the Project Camp I already knew what to improve/change	35.2%	23.5%
The Project Camp has changed my initial idea for the event	18.9%	14.4%
Despite the criticisms/suggestions, I prefer not to change anything about the idea presented	18.0%	2.0%
I will pay attention to the criticisms/suggestions made and analyse how they can contribute to improving the project developed	27.9%	60.1%

Projects' success rate of implementation has ranged from 67% to 100% over the years, demonstrating that students can successfully implement their events. However, the 2019/2020 academic year was atypical due to the COVID19 pandemic as students were unable to implement the events due to the emergency remote teaching-learning system imposed in the 2nd semester following lockdown measures. Additionally, students' approval rate in all EMLM's curricular units is high, ranging from 84% to nearly 100%, both in 2018/2019 and 2019/2020.

6. Plans to further develop the initiative

The EMLM has undergone continuous adaptations and improvements since its inception. The lecturers who develop this initiative are in constant search for formats that are more in tune with the reality of the labour market, especially at a time of deep uncertainty and constant transformation the events business is now facing and aim at increasing the EMLM's notoriety in tourism and hospitality higher education and with the various stakeholders.

The 2020/2021 academic year will act as a turning point on how the planning and development of the various moments of this learning model are carried out, both in terms of the proximity between students and lecturers, but mainly in terms of the tools used and work methodology. The events sector is now undergoing what is probably the most remarkable transformation experienced so far. The changes that all the moments of the "construction" of an event go through are profound, from conception to evaluation, and far exceed the commonly required skills for an event planner, leading us to believe that the future will be more short-term and that specific measures need to be implemented. Under the EMLM, we should, therefore:

i. Continue to disseminate this teaching-learning model to ensure it is widely used and tested. This way, we will be able to continue to apply an up-to-date methodology, adapted to the reality of the labour market and of society in general.

ii. Involve more curricular units so that students feel the real complementarity of contents and can maximise their knowledge in a transdisciplinary way.

iii. Aim at creating, right from the Idea Camp, a link with ESHTE's *alumni*, by selecting a group of former students, already in the labour market, who can mentor each of the student teams; we believe that the connection with the labour market and the creation of bonds with newcomers to the events businesses will give students a broader view of what the near future holds.

iv. Introduce an initial pitch at the Idea Camp stage where student teams present their ideas, thus creating a learning moment about the various concepts and choosing the best idea; each team would have the opportunity to understand how quickly the labour market reacts to new ideas and the importance of summarising and highlighting the event's value proposition.

v. Identify, from the very beginning, the digital skills and tools that can be used in all stages of the project since events are becoming highly technological environments and students should be familiar with the various tools that they have at their disposal.

vi. Strive to invite experts who represent the sector, not only for their experience but also in their ability to invest in students' projects. For instance, granting a financial incentive to the best project elected by the jury could add healthy competitive dynamics.

vii. Improve the dynamics of debriefing, involving students, lecturers, and *alumni*, and creating an action plan for the phase of project implementation.

viii. Call for diversification by encouraging the exploration of the various hybrid solutions available in the events sector and the different formats that have become part of the events lexicon in recent years.

The *Event Management Learning Model,* therefore, illustrates how uncertainty can serve as an encouragement for new thoughts, beliefs, and performances: "an opening to the possible", in Beghetto's words (2020). Indeed, genuine uncertainty generates new ideas and behaviours since "former ways of thought and action no longer serve us" (p. 2). In addition, this condition of uncertainty may also help students deal with anxiety and develop essential transversal skills such as autonomy, critical thinking, and problem-solving. This also helps lecturers, on the other hand, to acknowledge that learning processes are not linear and that many interesting possibilities can arise from uncertainty, thus challenging some of their expectations and preconceptions about learning and teaching. The EMLM thus offers a structured opportunity to fully embrace uncertainty and doubt as catalysts for learning and for the development of entrepreneurial skills that require both learners and learning facilitators to leave their comfort zone and to think and act differently. The pandemic context has only reinforced was already being required from education for some years, albeit in more subtle ways.

References

Beghetto, RA 2020, 'Uncertaint', in V Glăveanu (ed.) *The Palgrave Encyclopedia of the Possible,* Palgrave Macmillan, Cham. https://doi.org/10.1007/978-3-319-98390-5_122-1.

Dilts, RB 1994, *Strategies of Genius,* vol 1, Meta Publications, Capitola, California.

Idea Camp (whole concept): credits to the European Cultural Foundation and all the Connected Action for the Commons network of hubs: Culture 2 Commons (Croatia), Les Têtes de l'Art (France), Oberliht (Moldova), Platoniq (Spain), Krytyka Polityczna (Poland) and Subtopia (Sweden). All materials are licensed under CC-BY-SA: https://creativecommons.org/licenses/by-sa/4.0/

IdeaCamp 2015 co-creation materials v.2: © by Platoniq and Subtopia over the bases of the 2014 v.1 version (© by Platoniq, Subtopia and Les Têtes de l'Art). CC-BY-SA: https://creativecommons.org/licenses/by-sa/4.0/

Author Biographies

Susana Filipa Gonçalves has undertaken PhD research about gender in events management and holds a post-graduation in Higher Education Pedagogy. As a senior lecturer at ESHTE she teaches various subjects related to Events Management and is an integrated researcher at CiTUR – Centre for Tourism Research, Development and Innovation.

Ana Gonçalves is a senior lecturer at ESHTE, where she co-coordinates and teaches at the Arts, Humanities and Foreign Languages department. She is a senior researcher at the Centre for Geographical Studies (IGOT-ULisboa). She holds a post-doc in Geography and a European PhD in Literary and Cultural Studies.

Elsa Correia Gavinho holds a PhD in Tourism Spatial Planning and is an Invited Professor at the ESHTE, in the scientific area of Tourism and Leisure. Outside academia, she was the founder, co-owner and managing partner of a specialised company in adventure and nature tourism.

Francisco Silva has a PhD in Geography, is a specialist in Travel and Leisure, a senior lecturer at ESHTE and a senior researcher at the Centre for Geographical Studies (IGOT-ULisboa). He has been a photojournalist, works as a consultant in tourism, and is a trainer in several adventure activities.

Victor Alves Afonso holds an MBA and is a Specialist in Administration and Management. He is a Marketing and Finance Trainer, a Financial Analyst and a Certified Accountant. He is an adjunct professor at ESHTE and owner of a consulting company

Cláudia Lopes is an invited senior lecturer at ESHTE, in the scientific area Tourism and Leisure where she teaches events-related curricular units both at the undergraduate and master's degrees. She is also a founding partner of a corporate event management company.

Innovation Program for Digital Leaders

Victoria Harrison-Mirauer (MA Cantab, MSc), Professor of Practice Innovation & Strategy
Hult Ashridge Executive Education, Hult International Business School, Berkhamsted. UK

Victoria.Harrison-Mirauer@ashridge.hult.edu

Abstract: This case concerns a digital innovation program led by Hult Ashridge Executive Education for a leading global technology company with the objective of creating a cohort of innovative, entrepreneurial digital 'change agents'; it is anticipated these digital leaders will help to unlock innovation and entrepreneurship and drive digital transformation across the group. The program is a blended design including virtual workshops, reverse mentoring, business innovation projects and interaction with start-up companies. The program, now in its second year, has been described as highly impactful by participants and by key organisation stakeholders and the organisation has increased its investment, doubling the number of participants taking part in cohort 2. Impact is driven by the combination of internal organisation support, coaching and reverse mentoring, external input, faculty workshops and opportunities for participants to experience a strategic innovation project.

Keywords: innovation, digital transformation, innovation projects, digital innovation

1. Introduction

The digital leaders' program was designed to build a cohort of future leaders empowered to drive the organisation's innovation and digital transformation. Specifically, the program objectives were to build digital innovation capability through training in concepts and tools, participating in challenges and working on innovative digital business model ideas, create change agents /digital ambassadors who act as catalysts for change and innovation in local business units, and to use reverse mentoring to close generational gaps, enhance innovative mindsets and digital 'savviness, and foster a culture of inclusiveness and collaboration.

The program participants become alumni and continue to be involved in subsequent programs over time, with the aim of building a shared language and common practice across the organisation. The alumni act as 'go to' people for new ways of working in diverse teams across the business and have the support of their respective line managers to do so. This program forms part of a digital 'culture push' and is aimed at aspiring leaders who want to hone their learning agility, innovation capability and to drive technology led, customer centric solutions. Participant selection is through nomination by line management in accordance with the organisation's talent development frameworks. The program is described as being for participants interested in innovation and digital transformation but whose job role might be outside those disciplines. Participants were asked to complete an application letter outlining their experience and interest in digital innovation and what they hoped to gain from the learning.

The program design focuses on developing an innovative leader mindset including:

- Managing in uncertainty
- Tolerance of ambiguity
- Able to flex between expansive and reductive thinking at different times
- Learning /growth mindset
- Willingness to experiment
- Embrace diversity – of thinking, of approach, using stimulus, using environment
- Challenge assumptions
- Inspiring others

Specific participant learning outcomes include:

- Broadening capability to innovate and drive digital transformation
- Open mind to global trends, case studies and disruptive approaches
- Develop leadership skills including influencing and networking across the organisation and beyond the boundary of the firm
- Enhance learning agility and 'digital mindset'
- Gain exposure to successful business leaders internally and work with start-ups externally on strategic business challenges
- Exposure to innovation and intra-preneurship methodologies, case studies and practitioners
- Become part of an alumni group of change makers driving the organisation future.

2. The Infrastructure
Program Components:

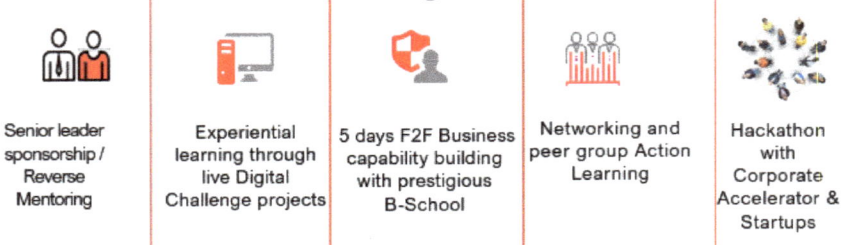

Figure 1: Innovative digital leadership learning journey, 9-12 months

The 12-month program learning journey includes: face to face and virtual workshops, 1:1 reverse mentoring, cross functional team strategic innovation project work and opportunities to interact with start-up eco system, supported by a virtual learning platform with learning resources and action learning sets. In light of travel restrictions, the second cohort of the program started with the virtual workshop elements branded 'Accelerators', followed by a 4-day residential and virtual project work and presentations. The reverse mentoring and project work, alongside access to a curated playlist of self-guided study materials available on the Hult Ashridge *Leadership Live* platform underpin learning for duration of the program. Leadership Live offers participants access to materials on specific topics, and the opportunity to explore leadership development areas specifically relevant to their individual needs.

3. Key people and brief role description:
Hult Ashridge Executive Education: Program designed and delivered by Hult Ashridge Executive Education Faculty. Program Director, Victoria Harrison-Mirauer, Professor of Practice Innovation & Strategy and Adjunct Faculty MOK O Keeffe.

Client Organisation; ABB Group is a leading global technology company numbering over 105,000 employees operating across 100 countries. ABB operations are organised into four global business areas, which in turn are made up of 20 divisions. Organisation team included L&D and HR leaders at the organisation as the core team and 6 senior project sponsors and participant mentors. The program was sponsored by a member of the ABB

Group Executive Committee and supported by a senior group of project sponsors.

Participants: Cohort 1 included 18 early-mid-career leaders with an interest in innovation and digital transformation. Line managers and sponsors nominated participants and supported them with time for projects and opportunities to 'teach back' post program at the local level. Cohort 2 included 55 early- mid career leaders.

Program Executive Sponsor: as the pilot program, cohort 1 was designed in collaboration with an executive sponsor who advised on program objectives and desired organisation outcomes. Alongside the project sponsors, the executive sponsor attended the virtual program kick-off and the innovation presentations workshops and provided end to end Executive level support for the program.

Reverse Mentors: senior business leaders in the organisation each committed to three reverse mentoring sessions of approximately 90 minutes, 1:1 with a participant. This process *reverses* the traditional mentoring and instead encourages the more senior person to learn from the 'digital native' in discussions on key innovation, digital transformation and leadership challenges. All innovation project sponsors participated in reverse mentoring.

Senior Innovation Project Sponsors: Senior leaders were invited to propose an innovation project or challenge for the participant teams to work on, and to act as sponsor for. They each completed a project brief- including a description, why this challenge matters to the business now, and a high-level scope. Innovation project sponsors were involved in briefing the participant project teams, and one sponsor attended the start-up 'hack day' during the residential, staying into the evening to join participants for an informal dinner to discuss the challenges and the program. Innovation project sponsors connected with their respective project teams on a regular basis and attended the final projects presentations workshop. Several innovation project sponsors continued to support alumni beyond the program. Project sponsors have been extended to include 6 senior leaders in cohort 2.

Innovation Project leaders: acting as a 'day to day' project mentor , this role is a Subject Matter Expert for participant project teams to call on for information, data, resources, connection and context.

L&D /HR team: Key stakeholders and drivers of the program internally, responsible for program management on the organisation side, and for supporting both the participants and sponsors /mentors in their roles and responsibilities. Also responsible for tracking impact internally, evaluation and creating conditions to nurture a network of alumni. Core team; Thomas Lienhardt, Talent and Learning Manager Electrification Business Area ABB, Ana Lundberg, VP Human Resources, Global HRBP Smart Buildings ABB and Annika Leist, Global HR Project Manager ABB.

Subject Matter Experts organisation side: for cohort 2 the Chief Innovation Officer and Chief Digital officer deliver 'Accelerator' virtual workshop sessions and an ABB group leader representing China operations shares a case study with participants interested in emerging markets and global strategy.

Hult Ashridge Executive Education Faculty: responsible for the design and delivery of the learning journey including; program design with L&D and HR team, inquiry with Executive sponsor and projects sponsors, leading workshops, briefing Hack day session and speakers, running Action Learning sessions and project support between workshops and modules, and using feedback to iterate design for future cohorts.

Hult Ashridge Adjunct Faculty Experts: experts within the Hult Ashridge adjunct faculty network host virtual 'Accelerator' workshops on topics including Agile Working and Industry 4.0.

Hult Ashridge Program support: responsible for program logistics face to face and virtually to ensure timings, logistics and technical support in place for program to run smoothly. Point of contact for participants.

Outside in- speaker and Technology Startup Accelerator Co:Cubed London: Ashridge partnered with Co:Cubed London, a corporate accelerator led by Jeremy Bassett, ex Unilever. Jeremy is briefed on the innovation challenges and participant projects and uses his network to bring start-ups working on relevant technologies to the 'hack' session. Jeremy also shares his own experience of the challenges bringing innovation to the 'core' of a large multinational blue chip.

3.1   Software /Platforms:
Microsoft Teams- virtual meetings, presentations and workshops using Microsoft Teams

Canvas – Hult Ashridge online platform where participants access program information timetables, faculty biographies, workshop pre-reading and program materials.

Leadership Live – Hult Ashridge Virtual Learning Environment with curated playlists of digital resources covering leadership, strategy, innovation, and topics relevant to the program learning outcomes.

In addition, the client organisation IT department provides a list of virtual collaboration tools, customer facing tools and technical tools for creating digital prototypes with information including what the tool is useful for, how to access and where to find appropriate training and support. Cohort 1 participants were encouraged to use these tools in particular on their project work and to experiment with new platforms and share their experiences with their peers. The impact of Covid-19 on cohort 2 renders these collaboration tools even more important.

3.2 Psychometric assessment and innovation diagnostic:

Me^2 general factor of creativity assessment; Me^2 covers 12 dimensions of creative problem solving. Individual reports *and* project team group reports are used to help individuals identify areas for development, team gaps and preferences. The Me^2 general factor of creativity is an online, self-report questionnaire designed to assess a person's preferred style of thinking, feeling and behaving in relation to creativity.

Korn Ferry Digital Success Leadership profile and assessment: cohort 2 used the Korn Ferry Digital Success profile and assessment at the beginning of their program to allow participants to benchmark their personal opportunities for learning and development over the course of the program in line with this leadership profile. The profile was deemed a deliberate 'stretch' for some, but in line with the program objectives to build 'change agents' able to drive innovation and digital transformation across the organisation.

Innovation Eco-System Diagnostic an online diagnostic which covers 4 dimensions of innovation in the organisation's innovation 'eco system'; Direction, Environment, Enablers, and Engine. All participants complete the diagnostic in relation to their area of the business and a report is provided for comparison and discussion.

Combined, these diagnostics offer an individual, team and organisation level view on innovation, and creative problem solving. The Me^2 assessment is accompanied by a range of exercises for individuals and teams to use to increase their capabilities in particular areas across the spectrum of activities from idea generation through to implementation in creative problem-solving contexts. The assessment focuses on skills which can be honed and learned and provided a useful snapshot for project teams. The teams were asked to review their individual and collective scores, to identify areas where they had gaps and to support individuals to develop strengths in areas they felt were deficient. One group in particular supported an individual to build her confidence in sharing ideas and another group modified their approach realising their high scores in the 'competitive' Me^2 domain might mean they were at risk of not incubating initial ideas for long enough. Providing some context for creative and complex problem-solving tendencies and preferences was a useful foundation for the teams as they approached their project work together. The participants asked if they could retake the assessment at the end of the program to see if their respective scores had improved. This will be taken into consideration for future cohorts.

Figure 2. Me^2 General Factor of Creativity. E Metrixx Ltd. (October 2013)

4. Program Content /Design

Program duration 9-12 months

4.1   Pre-launch:

Preparation materials: a range of reading and viewing materials were loaded into online learning platform and playlists on Ashridge Leadership Live were curated for participant asynchronous learning.

Innovation Projects and project sponsor briefing: projects were agreed with senior stakeholders and written up into project briefs for participants. Projects were chosen to be open ended, important and relevant to the business strategic and innovation goals, and to be rooted in the digital transformation agenda.

Participant selection and application- participants were proposed by line managers and selected based on organisation talent profiles. A *pdf* flier describing the program, learning objectives and candidate profile was produced to share across the organisation to aid the selection process. Participants were invited to submit 500 words about their suitability and intentions /learning opportunities in attending the program. Candidates were selected by the client team and project groups configured for diversity across geography, role / function and experience.

Program Outline

Interviews /inquiry with stakeholders	Informed program design and learning outcomes
Virtual learning platform	Set up with playlists for asynchronous learning
Psychometric	Me2 General Factor of Creativity online with individual reports and project team reports. Korn Ferry Assessment (cohort 2 only)
Innovation Eco System Diagnostic	Organisation level view across 4 dimensions
Projects set up and teams allocated	Project sponsors and leaders briefed and projects written up into project team briefs for participants
Virtual Launch	Whole cohort including senior stakeholder
Project team workshops	Individual project sponsors with respective project teams
Reverse Mentoring	1:1 participant and mentor, 3-4 meetings over program duration

Accelerators	Subject matter expert workshops (Virtual)
Residential module	5 days Ashridge House, UK and Co:Cubed Accelerator London
Project Action Learning x 3	Faculty led sessions with each project team x 3 over duration of program
Project work	Project teams working independently
Presentations /close	Presentations from all teams with all sponsors and program stakeholders (Virtual)

4.2 Program Content Highlights:

- Digital Innovation Landscape
    - Context for digital transformation and innovation, drivers of digital disruption, opportunities for the client organisation, the Innovation Eco System diagnostic, STEEP digital 'futures', Innovation and 3 Horizons Model, adapted from Baghai, Coley, White, (1999)

- Design Thinking and Agility
    - Design Thinking simulation on system level challenge , Empathy, Define, Ideation, Prototype, Test methodology (Kelley 2001), (Storvang, Haug, Nguyen 2020), (Doorley et al 2018) , user centricity, connected thinking, agile mindset and behaviours, Jobs to be Done theory (Ulwick 2016), various case examples including Intuit's Design for Delight approach.

- Hack day with start-ups- start-up pair matched with each innovation project team
    - Case study evolution of corporate innovation with Jeremy Bassett CEO Co:Cubed
    - Story of my start-up –founders' backstories, overview of their technology, and ambitions for the future.
    - Examinations- clients split into teams to interview one of the start-ups and Jeremy Basset to better understand how they set up, got going with a structured approach- topics including: where the idea came from, support received, trials and challenges, raising capital etc.
    - Making innovation happen and the role of low-cost experiments.

- o Collaborative innovation session in start-up teams.
- o Debrief and discussion on learning transfer into organisation and projects.
- Developing a digital mindset
  - o Build- measure-learn principles and approaches (Ries 2017).
  - o Working with direction, pace and an experimental mindset.
- Innovating the business model- Lego Serious Play
  - o Using Lego Serious Play approach to investigate current reality, agents acting on the system, disruption and future business models.
- Digital disruption and the 'innovator's dilemma'
  - o Theory of disruption, disruptive trends and the innovator's dilemma for large organisations (Christensen, 2016).
  - o Client organisation disruptor mapping.
  - o Strategies for dealing with disruption.
- Changing behaviours /change agent role in driving innovation

5. The Challenges

The innovation project approach initially met with some pushback from participants who worried about delivering on that commitment over and above their business-as-usual workloads. This resistance was overcome by a combination of senior project sponsorship, indicating the business was taking these projects seriously, and the allocation of a 'day to day' projects leader as subject matter expert to help guide questions and resources internally. In addition, participants were encouraged to negotiate individually with line mangers for time and support for their project work. It was a key part of the program design to deliberately leave this tension in play- innovation is often a 'fringe' or 20% time activity or an initiative over and above business-as-usual responsibilities. The program was designed to stay as true as possible to the realities of innovation and to expose participants to the challenges of 'intrapreneurship', so any resources required, meetings or connections needed, the participants were encouraged to work out for themselves. Specific focus on the need to 'influence without authority' was built into the design for cohort 2.

One group had a particularly challenging project with a large and undefined scope, their initial plan was predicated on a site visit and engagement with a particular business unit as a site for their pilot, this was halted by the pandemic restrictions and meant the team had to rethink. The process of reworking their project plan was a fantastic learning opportunity as they 'pivoted' to meet a new set of circumstances. The Action Learning Set style support sessions from Hult Ashridge faculty was central in keeping the project teams on track, it provided them with a safe and supportive space to explore options, express frustrations and to remind them of the learning as well as task – related outcomes.

The ability to influence without authority, and to start small, to fail fast and think about alternative approaches are central to the innovation capability and mindset objectives at the heart of the program. Challenges faced during project working were framed as opportunities to learn and experiment and participants are encouraged to use the innovation capability workshop frameworks and insights to help them identify and respond to these issues accordingly. These challenges reinforce the differences between innovation initiatives and 'business as usual' processes, with many participants looking for more guidance and timelines and deliverables at the outset of projects before recognising that the nature of innovation is in part to deal with a lack of initial guardrails.

Participants work in global project teams including participants from Europe, America and Asia, this creates challenges in terms of time zone, as well as the need to adapt to different working practices and cultures. The plan to meet in person for the innovation projects presentations at the end of cohort 1 was changed due to travel restrictions caused by Covid-19. The participants were unhappy not to meet in person for this part as they had formed strong bonds after the residential module. Efforts were made to build reflection time and social time into the workshops, and the need for connection and teambuilding was considered during the design phase for cohort 2 in 2021 /22.

6. How the initiative was received

Cohort 1 participants were asked to devise their own feedback sharing highlights and insights from their learning journey and this was shared with the group and with the senior organisation stakeholders at the program close. The participants were set a group task to collate feedback and insights and told this would be shared at the final innovation projects presentation workshop, the method and format for this was left to the group to determine for themselves. Cohort 1 nominated one member of each innovation project team and created an evaluation committee; they used a quantitative questionnaire and a video of qualitative reflections to collate feedback from all participants. Alongside this participant-led feedback, Hult Ashridge Executive Education provided a formal program evaluation survey which was completed by 80 % of the participants.

Highlights from the formal program evaluation include: positive response to the access to senior leaders and the opportunity through reverse mentoring to discuss business challenges and opportunities, high ratings of the face to face learning module at Ashridge House and the day spent at Co:Cubed office in London including interaction with start-up companies, working in cross functional and global teams and passion for the innovation initiatives and ideas presented.

"The LEGO session was very, very well done. It really stretched us to think broadly about our organization, how it operates, and how it could be greatly improved. It was also very interesting to work in that medium because I am typically telling stories using PowerPoint and spreadsheets rather than physical components."

"The program was very intense and full of content. There was a good balance between lessons and practical exercises. Overall the result and quality of the training is very good."

"I was a little sceptical coming in with how little information we had, but that was quickly taken care of on the first day. The experience at Ashridge helped me realize which parts of digital innovation my team and I already do well, and which parts need some focus and improvement."

"The digital innovation course at Ashridge introduced us to a new way of working and encouraged us to become change agents when we return to our day jobs"

"All of the senior leaders we came in contact with over the course of the week [face to face at Ashridge] were interested not only in the program, but in us as individuals. They all did a great job of building us up and stressing the importance of what we are doing in this program." (Source: Hult Ashridge Program Evaluation)

7. The Learning Outcomes

Business impact- all 4 business projects in cohort 1 were completed and presented to the executive committee, sponsors and stakeholders; the feedback at the workshop and beyond has been extremely positive, the Executive stakeholder and senior sponsors congratulated the participants on their learning and ideas. Cohort 2 are completing projects at the time of writing and project work has extended across a broader spectrum of organisation challenges.

One of the 4 projects in cohort 1 significantly changed the direction of an existing program underway with a big 5 consultancy in the organisation, the other projects created recommendations which are now being implemented in their respective business units.

Support for the program across the senior leadership team remains strong and the appetite for reverse mentoring as a means of culture change and innovation meant this experimental approach continued into cohort 2 and into other learning and development initiatives.

All participants ran 'teach back' sessions at the local level sharing their insights and learning after the face-to-face module this cemented the involvement of line managers and meant the learning was shared across the business divisions.

Participants created their own 'digital ambassador manifesto' outlining what the organisation would 'See', 'Hear' and 'Experience' differently as a result of their learning journey and the program, and they captured the essence of this with a slogan *'Start small, think big, act fast'* (Figure 3.).

Participants confirmed as high potential 'talent' continue to be tracked by L&D talent managers and line managers mindful of future career and leadership development opportunities. Evaluations of the program indicate high levels of satisfaction with all participants somewhat or extremely satisfied and an NPS of 71.43% Participants from cohort 1 were keen to offer feedback and to be involved as alumni for program cohort 2.

Figure 3. Digital ambassador

8. Plans to further develop the initiative

The initial program was commissioned for a second cohort into 2022. The organisation doubled the number of participants taking part, thereby extending the reach to include participants from newly acquired divisions of the ABB group.

Input from the 'inside out' including the participation of the organisation's Chief Innovation Officer and Chief Digital Officer is an addition for cohort 2 to ensure the context for innovation is relevant and current. The program is focussed on disruptive thinking and innovation beyond R&D so context is particularly helpful for participants in aligning the program work to the organisation innovation strategy.

The impact of alumni participation in cohort 2 is important– both in delivering the objective of building a community of practice and in extending the network of change agents further but also in how the alumni can input meaningfully to the learning. Alumni feedback on particular aspects of the program was incorporated into the design for cohort 2.

A session on the organisation view of what it means to be innovator and change agent led by the organisation's L&D leaders was incorporated at the beginning of cohort 2, alongside a session on 'influencing without authority'. This latter challenge is central to innovation initiatives where there is no clear roadmap or obvious line of authority, and where agile teams need to network across organisation silos.

In cohort 2 we have more time to ensure the start-up companies the groups meet with at Co:Cubed are aligned with the innovation project challenges, it is anticipated this will increase the emphasis in the 'hack' session on opportunities for co-creation.

We continue to review the use of collaborative software tools beyond Microsoft Teams- e.g mural.com and miro.com. The organisation's IT team have agreed to lend their support to project teams wanting to deploy innovative technologies to create prototypes such as *appypie* for app prototypes. This will enhance the project outputs and give the participants exposure to the process of prototyping and testing for feedback.

We have included a session on building the business case for innovation into residential module for cohort 2- designed to extend the learning beyond introducing participants to the business model canvas /lean canvas frameworks. The importance of the business case for innovation ties into one of the key messages from the Co:Cubed workshop. Understanding the commercial context is key to the eventual implementation of innovation and intrapreneurial initiatives.

Key Learning:

Stakeholder Buy-In

The senior sponsorship and executive support and organisation alignment behind this program are crucial. Participants appreciate unique access to senior leaders which broadens their understanding of the organisation's important strategic objectives and approach to innovation.

The project sponsors encouragement to participants to be 'disruptive', 'brave' and to challenge assumptions, is supported by their openness to participate in reverse mentoring. Anecdotally both the seniors and the participants value the candid and innovative approach - with both parties learning something new. Reverse mentoring represents an important cultural shift for the organisation and is part of an expressed intent to question 'old ways' and create new behaviours more conducive to innovation.

Diversity

The global cohort and cross functional teams bring diverse and varied perspectives. This diversity of experience, geography and know-how adds value to the learning experience and to the program learning outcomes. This diversity was enhanced in the design for cohort 2 augmenting the input from both organisation experts and external experts in a series of 'accelerator' virtual sessions designed to bring perspectives from the 'outside in'. In addition to the diversity of the organisation teams, one project team on cohort 1 worked alongside an external consultancy project team and a project team on cohort 2 is working with a spin out from the Polytechnic of Milan on Blockchain technology solutions. This collaborative working reflects the broader trend in corporate innovation partnerships beyond organisation boundaries.

Innovation Projects

Projects are used to quickly replicate real -world innovation and intrapreneurship challenges. Framed as strategic challenges projects have a broad scope and participants are encouraged to be 'disruptive' in their approach. Participants are encouraged to take a 'user centric' view and building their Design Thinking capabilities proves a helpful precursor to their project work. Design Thinking is not currently widespread practice in the organisation and is a useful example of different ways to approach innovation. Innovation is never a straightforward undertaking, the challenges project teams face around scope in particular and tensions about resourcing and time provide helpful learning opportunities as the teams learn to navigate these.

Teach- back

Teach back sessions offer the dual benefit of engaging wider networks of people in the business and the ensuring on-going support and involvement of line managers. Teach back sessions saw the participants using insight and knowledge gained on the program applied to their home teams /divisions. The format for these was left to individual participants, a 'roadshow' format was particularly successful for the Italian teams where participants in the program were invited to participate in a number of division -wide strategy and digital transformation workshops.

Interpersonal Connection and the challenge of Covid 19

Acknowledging the on-going challenge of Covid.19, the design has also been adjusted to include more time for social connection, fun and reflection which can be run virtually to encourage networking and social connection across the cohort group. Undoubtedly the opportunity to meet face to face and bond over social time at Ashridge House was a positive for the first cohort. It is hoped the second cohort can also meet in person.

Psychological safety and the virtual working environment:

We acknowledge the difficulties presented by virtual working and continue to pay attention to the pressing need to create safe 'spaces' to question and reflect which support collaboration and innovation.

Acknowledgements: The success of this program is testament to the enthusiasm and effort of the participants, the unerring and organisation wide support from senior leaders across the ABB group and to the enthusiastic input of Hult Ashridge faculty, adjuncts and external partners in particular Co:Cubed London. Thanks also to the ABB Learning & Development and Human Resources teams for their collaborative approach and tireless hard work.

Resources and Assessments

ABB Group homepage https://global.abb/group/en

Co:Cubed London https://www.co-cubed.com/

Innovation Eco System Diagnostic www.innovationbeehive.com

Me2 Psychometric https://ptc.bps.org.uk/test-review/me2-general-factor-creativity

References

Baghai, M., Coley,S., and White,D., (1999). *The Alchemy of Growth*, New York: Perseus Publishing.
Brown, T., *Change by Design*,(2019). Harper Business
Doorley et al., (2018). *Design Thinking Bootleg* available at https://dschool.stanford.edu/resources/design-thinking-bootleg alongside resources at www.ideo.com
Kelley, T., (2001). *The Art of Innovation*, New York, Broadway Books

Storvang, P., Haug, A., & Nguyen, B., (2020). 'A typology of strategies for user involvement in innovation processes', *Prometheus*, vol. 36, no. 4

Ulwick, A., (2016). *Jobs To Be Done*, Idea Bite Press

Author Biography

Victoria Harrison-Mirauer MA (Cantab) MSc is Professor of Practice and practice lead for Innovation at Hult Ashridge Executive Education. Victoria has led global innovation programs for a range of blue chips and spent 7 years of her 20 year career in the MENA region latterly as Head of Digital Strategy for the Abu Dhabi F1. Victoria commences her PHD at Cambridge University in 2021.

Demonstrator Lab: Where Entrepreneurial Academics Become Academic Entrepreneurs

Davide Iannuzzi and Eva C. Janssen
VU University Amsterdam, Netherlands

d.iannuzzi@vu.nl

1. Introduction

The Demonstrator Lab (DLab, www.demonstratorlab.nl) at Vrije Universiteit Amsterdam (VU Amsterdam) is an experimental entrepreneurship laboratory that gives students the opportunity to develop entrepreneurial skills or to share know-how with peer entrepreneurs. The lab offers a hands-on, risk-free, failure-free environment for the earliest phase of the idea-to-market process. Any student is welcome to join, as long as they are ready to get their hands dirty and not afraid to fail.

DLab offers budding entrepreneurs five key resources.

- **Infrastructure**, including office space, meeting rooms, and laboratory facilities.
- **Cash**, with no-strings-attached seed funding of up to €15,000, plus as much as €40,000 more if a project gains traction.
- **Mentorship**, in the form of professional coaching and peer feedback.
- **Community**, thanks to the strong ties between groups, who share space, problems, and solutions.
- **Connections**, through our extensive and proactive network, including potential investors.

DLab is a teaching facility in disguise. At first sight it may look like some kind of academic incubator programme but peering deeper you see it actually focuses on student education rather than return on investment. We operate at the very earliest stage of the innovation funnel and so make virtually no selection at intake; there is no cut on project scalability and we do not even select on the basis of the skills the team comes with at the start.

Figure 1. What the Demonstrator Lab has to offer

Unlike standard academic incubators, in fact, we do not want to help students *across* the valley of death. Rather, we take them from their eureka moment to the *edge* of the valley. From there, others can take over. Not all make it that far. In fact, most do not. But everyone ends up with a new set of valuable skills and something unique to add to their CV. DLab is as much about the journey as the destination!

One important detail is that DLab is open not only to students but also to researchers. This creates a melting pot where people of different ages, professional experience, and cultural backgrounds can interact and learn from each other with no hierarchical barriers. Peer-to-peer feedback is facilitated at regular user meetings, held in a common space called the Breakout Room. Take a 360° look here: https://youvis.it/yYSNMs

Figure 2. Academic entrepreneurs enjoying lunch in the Breakout Room.

Since 2017, DLab has supported hundreds of students and more than 90 different projects in a broad spectrum of sectors. All but 27 are still ongoing, and 18 have moved from idea to registered start-up. Our projects have secured external grant funding totalling in excess of €1.3 million, excluding external investment capital. This success has already caught the imagination of many in Amsterdam, where DLab has become a best-practice example of how to introduce entrepreneurship education at the academic level with a tool that eventually creates not only skills for students but also new wealth, jobs, services, and products for our society. Not surprisingly, other universities are now reaching out to copy our winning formula.

2. The infrastructure

The Demonstrator Lab is a learn-by-doing, multidisciplinary environment open to participants from all fields of study. Coaching, office space, facilities, networking events, and mentorship are provided free of charge to virtually any team of students interested in joining us. Since our focus is the educational aspect, not financial returns, we are effectively non-selective.

The strength of DLab stems from active engagement with the research community and from the ability to access a wealth of facilities – a comprehensive physical, intellectual, and financial infrastructure, not only in the scientific domain but also in such areas as product development (e.g., fast prototyping). As an interfaculty facility, we attract students and researchers from all sorts of backgrounds, from STEM to business, law to movement sciences and psychology.

From the product development point of view, risk is mitigated by exploring multiple scenarios to bring ideas out of the lab and into the real world with the backing of well-connected professionals. We provide opportunities to carry out a conceptual or technical feasibility study, for example, along with an analysis of the business case.

Participants gain access to state-of-the-art amenities on the VU Amsterdam campus, including 200 square metres of lab space equipped with all sorts of experimental and fabrication equipment. For prototyping, for instance, they can use the fabrication laboratory – a facility fully equipped with 3D printers, 3D scanners, a laser cutter, and a tabletop CNC machine, plus various mechanical and electrical tools. We can then refer them to the electronic and mechanical workshop operated by the Faculty of Science, where skilled professionals support groups on more complex projects.

Office space, meeting rooms, and ancillary facilities bring the total extent of the DLab physical infrastructure to 580 square metres. This forms an integrated environment, as practical as it is academic, dedicated to stimulating entrepreneurship.

Figure 3. At work in DLab office space.

Guidance services like mentoring and coaching are tailored to individual needs and wishes, following a deliberately informal, non-structured approach. Within this invigorating setting, participants work on the functional features of their concept whilst at the same time receiving advice and support in all aspects of the idea-to-market process from peers, management, and our professional network.

The Demonstrator Lab is equipped to guide the budding entrepreneur throughout that trajectory: from forming a team to developing a prototype; from working out the most efficient marketing strategy to finding the resources needed to put it into practice. DLab thus provides all the help a participant needs to explore whether their idea might just make it.

In line with effectuation theory of entrepreneurship, typical activities provided within this development framework include:

- analysing the resources and capabilities of the team and the surrounding environment;
- identifying the actual customer added value hidden in the team's abstract idea;

- fixing the team's goals and affordable losses;
- creating the network of collaborators (including first customers) needed to test the idea;
- building a prototype or minimum viable product (MVP);
- testing the prototype with customers; and,
- evaluating progress and designing a strategy to move forward.

In our flexible system, a process of this kind has no fixed outcome. It may lead to the creation of a new MVP, to a search for further funding, to the project being pivoted in a new direction or even to abandonment of the original idea and trying something else.

Community building is another pillar of the DLab concept. Our team connects participants with an extended network of academic, scientific, and commercial partners, with the worlds of business and applied science as a whole and in particular with the regional entrepreneurship ecosystem in and around Amsterdam. We also stimulate them to interact with other participants, and especially to connect with fellow students from different disciplines. In this respect, it is important to stress that the DLab has become a pole of attraction also for students who do not necessarily have a commercial idea themselves, but are still interested to offer support to existing projects by sharing their skills and know-how. We have for example started a collaboration with the International Master in Technology Law, whereby students from the law school team up with our groups to analyse potential roadblocks in the development of a given product or service. It is in fact not rare that a DLab project, led by students with a STEM background, suddenly has to tackle unexpected issues with term sheets, GDPR regulation, or product liabilities, to name a few. Students from the law school can apply what they are learning in their studies to a very concrete case. This kind of collaborations allows them to live, first hand, the rollercoaster of a start-up while advancing their communication, teamwork, and organizational skills. We have established similar connections with the School of Business and Economics and with the Bachelor and Master courses in Science, Business, and Innovation, and we are now launching another program whereby students involved in courses focused on sustainability will benchmark the DLab's projects with respect to the UN Sustainable Development Goals paradigm.

Our network consists of mentors, coaches, a variety of experts, business strategists, business angels, venture capitalists, market analysts and, last but not least, potential users of the proposed product or service. All these people, together with peers and colleagues, help the student entrepreneur to formulate a set of hypotheses and milestones and to perform tests with real customers. Crucially, every three or four months we check on how they are doing and decide with them whether or not the project is still worth proceeding with. Once a year we all gather at our Open Day, where our network comes together in a sort of start-up market. In 2020 this event took place online and attracted more than 140 participants. To expand our network further, we have recently started an alumni programme as well, whereby former students of the VU can join our meetings and act as mentors to our teams.

Importantly, the coaching infrastructure includes connections to scholars who regularly teach and perform research in entrepreneurship. The latter not only provide hands on advice, but also encourage our students to look into the theoretical aspects that better fit their project. In this way, our DLab students can accompany the hands-on experience with the study (and practical testing) of theories and methods discussed in the academic literature.

Peer-to-peer feedback is facilitated at regular user meetings held in a common space known as the Breakout Room. At these gatherings, student entrepreneurs discuss the challenges they face and share advice. Newcomers introduce their business idea and are brought up to speed with the DLab community, whilst outside professionals present their services. The wide variety of entrepreneurial journeys makes for an inspiring educational experience and encourages co-creation.

Last but by no means least, our financial infrastructure provides prospective student entrepreneurs with solid cash backing. Thanks to support from the City of Amsterdam, our teams can claim seed funding of up to €15,000. This comes with no strings attached and the application involves a minimum of bureaucracy. For a small, select group of projects which have proven their potential in the early stages, further flagship grants worth as much as €40,000 are available.

Clearly, a program of this kind could not develop well without the support of a robust management team, which is composed by academic researchers who have experienced the start-up process themselves and by business developers of the VU technology transfer office IXA (Innovation Exchange Amsterdam).

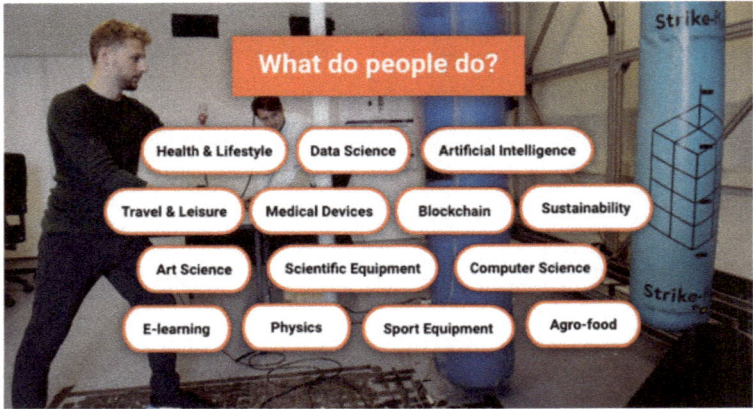

Figure 4. The DLab project spectrum.

All in all, then, the DLab infrastructure represents a unique development environment for students with an enterprising idea. We give them physical space in which to turn their concept into a tangible product, funds to buy the things they need, a range of coaching, mentoring, and peer support to build their entrepreneurial mindset as well as gather feedback on their business plans and, finally, access to our extended network of venture capitalists as well as potential users. Within this constellation of services and support, they choose what they need to take their idea from brainwave to reality.

3. The challenges

Like any new project launching in a cash-strapped academic environment, in its start-up phase the Demonstrator Lab struggled to achieve visibility amongst the VU Amsterdam community. Funds to publicise the initiative were extremely limited, so the team had to find low-cost and no-cost ways to generate awareness. One technique that proved particularly effective was direct engagement, taking every possible opportunity to break into classes and talk about DLab – a form of "guerrilla action" which appealed to students and highlighted the unconventional nature of the project. Students nursing entrepreneurial ideas, who previously did not know what do with them, were almost literally invited to abandon the classroom and bring their business concept to the new laboratory. In parallel, in collaboration with the School of Business and Economics, we have designed a whole series of courses that could introduce the basic principles of entrepreneurship to students of bachelor programs that very rarely engage with business oriented topics. These courses (which include "Entrepreneurship for Physicists", "Entrepreneurship for Biomedical Technology and Physics", "Entrepreneurship in Human Movement Science", and "Entrepreneurship in AI and Computer Science") consist of both academic lessons (focused on theory of entrepreneurship), soft skill development sessions (including networking, negotiation, and teamwork), and a project. For the latter, the students are grouped in small teams who, by the end of the course, must provide a complete business model canvas based on an original idea of them. The course coordinator then signals the best projects to the director of the DLab, who finally contacts those teams and explicitly invites them to join the lab. This formula proved to provide excellent projects, driven by highly motivated students. Likewise, the director of the DLab is in constant contact with the coordinators of the bachelor, master, and minor in entrepreneurship – another source of interesting projects led by interesting groups.

Inspiring active engagement with DLab and commitment to a project we are overseeing has created a second challenge: combining academic study with the development of a product and a business. There is always a danger that participants become so wrapped up in their entrepreneurial activities that they neglect their degree. To overcome this dilemma, the management team enforces the "credit points first" principle: our students know that we are aware of their academic commitments and that we expect them to put these before their start-up project. DLab is something they have to do alongside or after their standard curriculum, not instead of it. We have also developed formulas whereby students can work at DLab and earn credit points in return – a solution that can give a real boost to a project. Financing remains a constant challenge. So far we have been supported by the City of Amsterdam, which provides the cash contributions for the teams, and by VU Amsterdam, which covers our overheads. Our physical space is "borrowed" from Corporate Real Estate and Facilities, for example, whilst the Faculty of Science bears our management costs and the Innovation Exchange Amsterdam (IXA) takes care of PR on our behalf. We are now talking to the board of the university and the city government about further support for future activities, whilst also looking at other funding opportunities.

Over the past year, Covid-19 has forced our physical facilities to close. As far as possible, we have continued to offer coaching via Zoom and to hold regular online meetings with all our active project teams. We also gave some the opportunity to take their equipment, materials, and products home.

So far, the pandemic has not had any major effect with regard to intake. We have observed a detrimental impact on some weaker projects, though, due to the combination of a general dip in motivation and lack of contact time. But with on-campus activities severely affected by lockdown measures, overall we find that the collaborative environment we have created around DLab – our online community, for example – is now proving one of its great strengths. Despite the challenge, we have been able to "keep the ball rolling" through Covid-19 and to demonstrate that the organisation is resilient and ready to gear back up to speed as soon as restrictions are lifted.

4. How the initiative was received

What began as a modest pilot in the Department of Physics and Astronomy quickly expanded throughout the Faculty of Science and then to the Faculty of Behavioural and Movement Sciences and the School of Business and Economics. More recently we have seen greater participation from the Law School, and there are strong signals that we will soon be able to involve the Faculty of Social Sciences and the Faculty of Humanities as well. As word spreads, more and more students are realising that DLab represents a once-in-a-lifetime opportunity. Below are testimonials from just a handful of the hundreds of students who, spread across 91 different teams, have been participating in our programme.

> *"DLab is not just a sandbox for start-ups, not just a place where you get an office with a table and chairs, but a place where innovative and courageous ideas find early support. But most importantly, a place where extremely talented people meet to encourage and help each other out. Without its support we wouldn't be where we are today. DLab showed us how to come up with new directions every time we had a problem."*
>
> Elena Köstler, Niluk.App (MSc Cognitive Neuroscience/MSc Psychology)

> *"I can honestly say that DLab has changed my life. It's more than a place to learn, it's a doorway into the world of entrepreneurship. By combining theory and practice, I learnt how to make up a balance sheet and a profit-and-loss statement, and apply it to my own expenditure for product development. I also learnt electrical engineering and how to solder, how to pitch, how to implement my*

strategic plan, and – because DLab keeps offering amazing business opportunities on a daily basis – how to say 'no'."

> Jardo Stammeshaus, Liion Power (MSc Physics/MSc Science, Business and Innovation)

"At DLab we've been able to talk about our concept with other critical entrepreneurs and so develop the idea. Besides that, we've gained access to research possibilities and have thus been able to lay the foundation of Cupplement. DLab also supported the development of our MVP with its in-house knowledge and resources, even though we had no previous lab experience."

> Stefan Wateler, Cupplement (MSc Policy, Communication and Organisation)

"Since entering DLab we've realised a proof-of-concept setup of our system, formed a limited company and currently have a team of 14 full and part-time employees and interns. Last year we received our first government subsidy of €70,000 and joined HightechXL. Currently, we're filing our first patent and are raising more funding. As student entrepreneurs, DLab offered us space, budget, and support essential to getting our company off the ground and allowed us to learn about our technology, the market, and other aspects of building a business in a relatively risk-free manner."

> Nigel Visser, Veridis (MSc Entrepreneurship/MSc Advanced Matter and Energy Physics)

"With the help of DLab, we had the option to work in an entrepreneurial environment with other growing start-ups and learn from each other's best practices. Additionally, we were continuously connected to valuable people who helped RabbitQuest along its journey. Working at DLab enabled us to learn from experts about important start-up topics such as investor negotiations, and it gave us a steep learning curve by always having experienced sparring partners to talk to about different topics who also introduced us to an extremely valuable network."

> Gijs Limborgh, RabbitQuest NewU (MSc Human Movement Sciences)

Not everyone eventually succeeds. As a matter of fact, most projects do not reach the target market. The students who had been engaged in those projects, however, can still look back at a positive experience, where they learned skills and know-how that can hardly be acquired with standard in class lessons. In this respect, one could say that the DLab is the proof that, in entrepreneurship, there is not such a thing like failure.

> *"The demonstrator lab has not only provided us with the opportunity, guidance and resources to investigate the feasibility of our product and the possibility to bring it to the market. It has also taught us that beginning a startup encompasses way more than developing a good product. Unfortunately our product did not reach the stadium at which we could monetize on it, but the lessons we have learned on the way are incredibly valuable."*
>
> Vincent van der Meij, (MSc Astronomy and Astrophysics)

> *"The D-lab was the perfect place for us to try to all the things we wanted to get our start-up off the ground, with plenty of facilities, many other entrepreneurs to interact with and excellent advice and guidance [...]. Even though in the end the project did not take off, we have learned many invaluable things that can't be learned other than through experience."*
>
> David Hendriks, (MSc Advanced Matter and Energy Physics)

> *"Demonstrator Lab was a very valuable experience in my entrepreneurial career. Like many student entrepreneurs we didn't have a clue what we were doing at first, but with guidance and an available network from Demonstrator Lab, both on a personal level as well as during group presentations of our business, we received many valuable insights in how to start and validate our early stage business. In the end, our Demonstrator Lab venture did not make it very far on the market and seized operations, but the knowledge gained gave us the required ammunition to set out on new adventures."*
>
> Dan Zaat, (BSc Science, Business, Innovation)

> *"The support from the Demonstrator Lab has been very helpful; without it we would never have made it to the semifinals of the Phillips Innovation Award."*
>
> Isabelle van Keulen, (MSc Advanced Matter and Energy Physics)

DLab has been received with equal enthusiasm by our external stakeholders. The City of Amsterdam has praised our infrastructure as a best-practice example of hands-on education with societal relevance. Likewise, the professionals gravitating around DLab all recognise its impact, as witnessed by their commitment to stay connected. In collaboration with the University of Amsterdam (UvA), we are now going to open a DLab in the other main campus of the city; discussions with the Amsterdam University Medical Centre are under way to open at the academic hospital as well. Other universities in the Netherlands and abroad seem interested in our approach as well.

Figure 5. Gijs Limborgh (l) and Bart Spangenberg of health app _NewU_ , one of the 91 projects so far supported by DLab.

5. The learning outcomes

Demonstrator Lab has undergone rapid development since its establishment in 2017, and as summarised below has proven a resounding success.

- Number of projects supported: 91
- Number of students introduced to hands-on entrepreneurship: more than 200.
- Number of projects discontinued: 27.
- Number of start-ups: 18 (16 limited companies, two non-profit foundations).
- Grants: more than €1.3 million.
- Awards and honours (selected):
  - one Dutch Research Council Open Mind grant;
  - one project listed amongst the five most innovative start-ups in the Accenture Innovation Awards competition;
  - one project selected for the K-Start-up Grand Challenge programme in South Korea;

- two projects selected for the Academic Start-up Competition for the most ground-breaking Dutch research innovations, with one reaching the top 10 and thus being given the opportunity go to Silicon Valley to present its work;
- three IXA Innovation Awards;
- one semi-finalist in the Philips Innovation Award;
- one finalist in the Best Academic Start-Up award;
- one winner of the Dutch Sport Innovation Award;
- one recipient of an investment of €300,000 on the Dutch version of the TV show *Dragons' Den*.

Importantly, all discontinued projects have ended with a handshake and a group of grateful students. This, too, is a positive learning outcome: DLab is as much as about the journey as the destination. And even "failures" generate feedback providing valuable input for evaluations and analyses.

DLab's aim is to unleash the entrepreneurial potential of our organisation. In that sense, it has more than achieved its intended learning outcome.

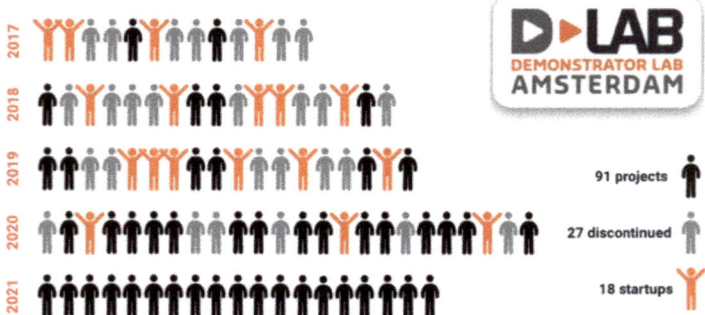

Figure 6. DLab projects, 2017-2020. In total, more than 200 students and staff have been introduced to entrepreneurship!

6. Plans to further develop the initiative

DLab has been growing and improving steadily since it was first set up nearly five years ago. We have reached a stable situation in which we can absorb as many projects as apply to us and still provide everyone with the support they deserve. Nevertheless, there is still plenty of room to improve our service. We have set ourselves a number of priorities for the next three years.

- Guarantee stable financial support to provide our teams with the resources they need and to cover our overheads.
- Cut inefficiency and professionalise our monitoring system, from entrance to exit.
- Continue to expand our community with an inclusive approach driven by common interest in the world of entrepreneurship.
- Continue to add peer-to-peer advisory services for our teams, involving more and more students from different disciplines across the VU Amsterdam campus.
- Build a web-based matchmaking platform to connect our teams with external professionals in our network.
- Position DLab in a wider context by working with all the other academic entrepreneurship initiatives in Amsterdam to create the best possible experience for our students.

Importantly, too, we will offer our support to any other organisation interested in reproducing our formula. For universities that wish to extend their entrepreneurship education, foster multidisciplinary collaboration, and achieve valorisation targets and ambitions, the DLab model pioneered at VU Amsterdam provides an effective, easy-to-implement solution. The concept has recently been adopted by our neighbours at the University of Amsterdam, who will soon have their own DLab location. Conversations with other universities in the Netherlands and abroad are currently ongoing. How exciting would it be to create a European Demonstrator Lab Network that keeps learning from the experiences accumulated by its members across the continent?

Author biographies

Davide Iannuzzi is Professor of Physics and head of its Demonstrator Lab, VU Amsterdam. He has a strong teaching track record and is author of nearly 100 publications. He has been awarded some €8m in funding, including four ERC grants

Eva Janssen is Program Manager at VU Amsterdam. With 7 years' experience as a freelance communications manager, she is skilled in growing concepts and building communities. After developing a successful summer school program, she is now on a mission to create a more entrepreneurial university.

Experiencing Innovation Led by Students

Michal Jirásek and Eva Švandová
Department of Corporate Economy, Faculty of Economics and Administration, Masaryk University
mijirasek@mail.muni.cz
eva.svandova@econ.muni.cz

Abstract: The initiative represents a newly created course Innovation Management. The course belongs to the core curriculum of the Master-level program Business Economics and Management. During its first iteration covered in this paper, the course was attended by 85 students. Due to the pandemic restrictions, teaching was delivered fully online. Despite the limitations, we stuck to the original plan of replacing the classical teacher-led model with the learner-led model. The course aimed to give students a comprehensive insight into innovations on two levels: individual/team and organizational. In the first case, students worked on a team project that simulated an innovation process in which students developed and tested a board game. In the second case, we let students understand strategic decision-making through case studies. From the feedback we continuously collected, we know that students very much appreciated the demanding yet very beneficial format of the course.

1. Introduction

"Tell me and I will forget; show me and I will remember; let me do it, and I will understand." (B. Franklin)

The Innovation Management course was not part of the university's curriculum previously. That gave us a free hand in its formulation that was led in the spirit of Benjamin Franklin's quote above: We intended to let students truly experience innovation, not just read or listen about it.

Based on this aim, we had in mind to give the course the following characteristics:

- Give students hands-on experience of innovations where possible.
- Let students experience the whole innovation process, including prototyping.

- Give students an understanding of selected innovation tools and methods – both at the individual/team and organizational levels.
- Give students free hand in work on their project as much as possible during seminars (small group sessions) while not imposing any restrictions on their work unless necessary.
- Create an environment that gives students the resources needed to do their work (study materials, feedback, advice and sufficient time) so they will be empowered to fully immerse in their innovative projects.

We worked with students on two levels of innovation management, which we considered important to achieve our aims: (1) Individual/team level, on which students worked in teams and experienced a product development journey. The assignment for the teamwork was to create a board game supporting the development of selected skills of the customer group. The whole process was managed by the stage-gate system in which members of a team also served as gatekeepers for another team's project. The learning from the project was regularly documented by students into a development portfolio, a collection of both outputs and reflections. (2) Organizational level, on which we used case studies of companies facing various strategic innovation challenges. On this level, we applied several strategic innovation tools and emphasized discussion and comparison of various students' ideas.

2. The infrastructure

2.1 Course organization

The course was taught by two teachers who are also the authors of this paper. Besides them, there were two external experts (one entrepreneur who shared his experience in a lecture; and one lecturer who led a workshop on Lean Business Canvas). Nevertheless, in the spirit of the course, a significant portion of the learning process was covered by 85 Master-level students who took part in the course.

The course took part in a 12-week semester with 2 teaching hours (100 minutes) of small-groups seminars every week and 2 teaching hours (100 minutes) of lectures every two weeks. In sum, there were 18 teaching blocks, most of them were characterized by either student-led activities (work on the project) or activities in which students played a major role (case studies). The breakdown is illustrated in Figure 1.

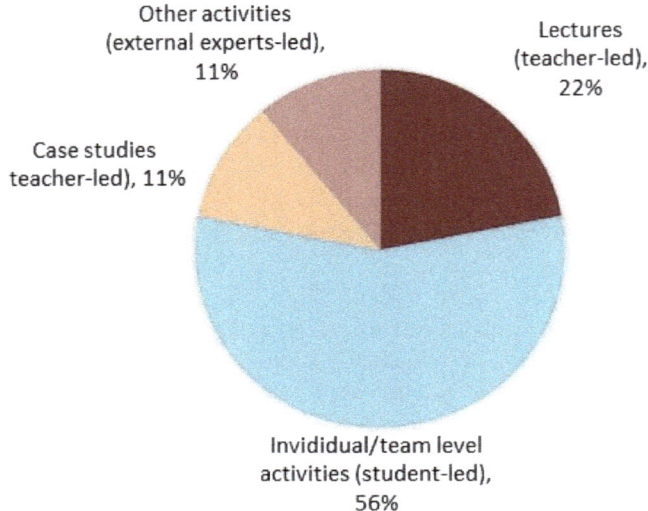

Figure 1. Breakdown of activities

Tools for communication and sharing

Due to the pandemic restrictions, the course was delivered fully online. We were using two main online tools. First, MS Teams served as a communication platform (for both synchronous and asynchronous communication) and document storage system. Initially, due to technical restrictions for breakout rooms MS Teams had in autumn 2020, we used the Zoom platform on several occasions to let students work in smaller groups during the seminars through breakout rooms.

Second, by the university bylaws, all the courses taught during the pandemic had to have detailed instructions in the university's information system in a form of an interactive syllabus. We decided to turn the obligation into an opportunity and we used this webpage as a universal information hub containing all the necessary information. This had been highly advantageous as instructions in the course were quite complex and complicated to comprehensively communicate through Teams. Information was be divided into two basic categories: (1) general information about the course (basic information, semester project, overview of methods and tools), and (2) information for each week (included teachers-written reflections of the previous week, materials for the lecture, materials for the seminar, assignment). As a part of the interactive syllabus, there were recordings of the lectures and a large number of pre-recorded videos and materials that covered the important concepts from innovation management in greater detail.

2.2 Course content

The dominant part of the course was dedicated to activities related to the individual/team level. This was a result of the time we gave students to work on their project, not a prioritization of this specific content.

We started lectures with the two lectures dedicated to the individual/team level in order to give students a quick briefing of over-arching concepts we planned to use during the semester (mainly innovation process and its stages, including core methods). Later, there were three organizational-level lectures (business model innovation, innovation culture, and innovation strategy). In between them, there was a workshop by an external consultant from the regional innovation center (JIC Brno) who went through Lean Business Canvas. To give students a real-life experience with innovations on an organizational level we also invited a speaker for an extra lecture in which he covered his experience with founding and developing a successful hardware start-up.

Small-group (around 28 students) seminars had three types of content: project teamwork (either with specific instruction or based on students' deliberation), evaluation gates (in which two student teams co-operated), and case studies. For case studies, we always split the class into two halves – one went in the first part of the session through the case study under the guidance of the teacher, the second went through another work. In the second part of the seminar, they switched. This way, students had enough opportunities to actively participate despite being in the online environment.

Individual/team level content

Three innovation management concepts that guided learning on this level were Innovation Pentathlon Framework (Goffin and Mitchell, 2017), Design Thinking, and Stage-Gate model (Cooper, 2017). From each of these concepts, we drew some inspiration but we did not attempt to fully cover them. Instead, we let their principles help students in the work on their team projects.

The prevailing part of seminars was devoted to the team project. Its goal was to develop a new board game. The choice of a board game as a theme was motivated by several reasons: the possibility to implement and absorb experience from the whole innovation process, including prototyping; the appeal of board games to both children and adults (meaning that virtually everyone has experience with playing); and a potential for commercialization (meaning that students could develop a business case). The examples from the students' work are contained below in Figure 2.

Figure 2. Examples of student's work

The innovation process was built upon the Stage-Gate model (Cooper, 2017), where each innovation stage is followed by a gate. At the gate, work from the stage is assessed and goals for the next stage are set. The timeline for the process was set by teachers, who also set basic requirements. However, the organization of gates as well as any additional requirements were left to students' discretion. Gatekeepers (another student team) were motivated to play an active role in the gate by sharing part of the final assessment of the evaluated project.

The actual teamwork started in the third week of the semester (during the first two weeks, students can unenroll from the course and, therefore, some teams were not stable yet) and ended one week before the end of the semester. The final week was devoted to peer review of a game created by a team from another seminar group. That simulated a game experience without previous knowledge of the game and its mechanics.

During the stages, students applied a wide range of innovative methods to finalize the project. There were four stages:

1. Getting to know the target group and generating ideas (3 weeks).
    a. Choice and analysis of the target group including a problem that the product should solve.
    b. Examples of creativity methods used by students (they weren't required to use all of them: brainstorming, brainwriting, Crazy 8, affinity diagram, SCAMPER, synectic, analogy, morphological analysis.
2. Selecting ideas for the game (2 weeks).
    a. Analysis of the board game market (focused on the similar target group and problem), creation of Lean Business Canvas.
    b. Selection methods: six thinking hats and voting.
    c. Attributes of a game and determination of the need to test them.
3. Prototyping and creating the first version of the game (2 weeks).
    a. Teams created their process to deliver a prototype that could be tested.
4. Finalizing the prototyping of the game (2 weeks).

a. Finalizing prototypes for peer-review, including testing with the target group.
b. Update of Lean Business Canvas and creation of Value Proposition Canvas.

From the second stage students also started working on a business case for the game by working on a Lean Business Canvas and later on Value Proposition Canvas.

Three gates separated the stages. The evaluated team created a self-assessment report in their development portfolio – both served as material for the assessment. During the gate, the evaluated team quickly presented its progress, received feedback on goal attainment from the evaluating team, and finally both teams jointly set goals for the next stage.

Each team continuously documented its activities and learning journey into a development portfolio. The development portfolio is a collection of study artifacts used for (self-)reflection and presentation. Besides containing outputs and records of the progress made by the team it was also a place for reflection. Students regularly reflected on their learning by answering to questions: What have we learned? What has failed and how to avoid it next time? What has been successful? The development portfolio served both the students in checking how their work progressed and what they learned and evaluators (gatekeepers and teachers) in providing feedback.

Organizational level content

The organizational level content was based on case studies. The core methods for this level were selected from Strategyzer's line of books: Business Model Generation (Osterwalder and Pigneur, 2010), Value Proposition Design (Osterwalder et al., 2015), and The Invincible Company (Osterwalder et al., 2020). The underlying theme behind choosing firms for case studies was to present students with three typical scenarios in which organizations may find themselves in the market and the challenges they present for strategic (business model) innovation:

1. A newly established, growing organization: Heaven Labs. Heaven Labs aims to revolutionize the food industry by introducing universal nutritionary-full food, Mana. With the case study, students worked on Business Model Canvas, personas, and Value Proposition Canvas.

2. An established company that wants to grow its business: IKEA. With the case study, students worked on Business Model Canvas, balancing exploration and exploitation, and mainly Blue Ocean Strategy (Kim and Mauborgne, 2015).
3. An established company facing market disruption: Disney. With the case study, students worked on Business Model Canvas, sustainable competitive advantages (VRIO, Barney, 1991), real options, and Portfolio map.

For case study work, every seminar group was then split into two parts: one worked with a teacher on a case study, while the other one on activities related to their team project. After half of the seminar (ca. 45 minutes), the students changed their roles. For every case study, there was a list of topics for students to prepare for. During the seminars, a teacher went through the topics in detail with a small group of students (10-15 participants). The emphasis was on the discussion and comparison of students' ideas. The goal was not only to focus on the hands-on understanding of methods but also on consequences of individual students' ideas, i.e., showing that numerous ideas can be valid (while many others are not meaningful) and how they impact subsequent decision making.

3. The challenges

The major challenge we encountered was the unplanned move of the whole course online. That limited us in realizing some activities we had prepared. Also, it presented a liability in communication and interactivity. In the case of individual activities, it was not difficult to prepare online alternatives. As for the online communication, we set a voluntary – yet repeatedly reminded – policy for "cameras on" that was adhered to by virtually all the students. We (teachers) also constantly explained the rationale behind individual activities and the whole course. That likely resulted in a high students' willingness to take part in the learning process. Finally, as the process was often student-led there were only a few opportunities to stay inactive.

Naturally, we faced numerous smaller challenges created by both the relative complexity of the course, its dissimilarity to ordinary courses students encountered at the university, and general setbacks caused by the online environment. We dealt with them on an ongoing basis, again with the emphasis on constant communication. Explanations and honest declarations of mistakes were the basic help in overcoming these issues.

Despite the pandemic and the challenges presented for education, we believe that we provided students with a fully-fledged learning experience. However, it is important to admit that the teaching burden was considerably high. Especially at the beginning when numerous adjustments had to be made with moving the course online. However, this was also connected with the fact that it was the first run of the course, so it was necessary to prepare all the materials from scratch.

4. How the initiative was received by the participants

During the course, we regularly collected (every week) feedback that served as an important touchpoint with the students' learning process. We used it also for continuous adjustment of some aspects of the course. Through this feedback, we know that the course was evaluated as time-consuming, but also extremely beneficial in learning key concepts of innovation management.

Our insights into students' evaluation of the course were later supported by an anonymous university-wide survey. In this survey students regularly evaluate all the courses on several pre-set items plus they may also add open comments. The most frequent positive comments appreciated: innovative course, innovative approach, interactive student involvement, absence of memorization, interesting content, or nice atmosphere. As for the negatives many places to share the information, time demands, and irregular feedback for the project were mentioned.

Figure 3 contains evaluation from the individual pre-set items.

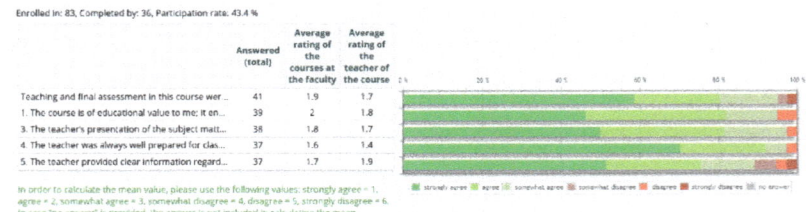

Figure 3. Results of the university-wide survey after the end of the semester

One important thing is to note the response rate which is usually around 10-20% of students. A twice as big response rate shows a high involvement of students in the course. Finally, the course was nominated by students for the rector's award for the best course in 2020.

5. The learning outcomes

The learning outcomes were evaluated on the same two levels as the content of the course:

1. **Individual/team level**. Grading criteria are very salient for the students at the university and we wanted to avoid them interfering with the learning process. For that reason, we evaluated the project mainly based on the work during the semester, not the outcomes (although we paid attention to the final product as well). As stated before, part of this evaluation was also shared by the group that was representing gatekeepers for the given team. The basis for the evaluation was the development portfolio. The learning outcomes were reflected either in project outcomes or in the regular reflection contained in the portfolio.

2. **Organization level**. The evaluation of this level was the basis of the final exam that took a form of a case study. Students received a case study one day before the exam and went through the exam in groups of three. Similar to in-semester case studies, the emphasis was put on the application of methods and argumentation for own ideas. Interaction between teacher and students provided a very good insight into their understanding of the methods and concepts connected to this level.

Overall, we believe that students got not just understanding but also hands-on experience with all the core methods mentioned above (in the Course content part of the text). From the point of view of specific competencies students can now apply a broad range of innovation methods; realize their benefits and implementation drawbacks; understand the innovation process and individual stages; create, understand, and apply strategic decisions related to innovations.

6. Plans to further develop the initiative

We plan to continue with the two-level structure of the course. On the level of cases, we will probably stick to three cases through the semester. We will consider having one of these cases span not only one but two seminars to offer students a possibility to build directly on previous insights.

On the team project level, we plan to clearly distinguish between methods we consider core for students (as future innovators) to master and methods that are optional. With core methods (e.g., Business Model Canvas, Stage-

Gate model) we plan to work more regularly so that students will get used to them. However, we intend to select only a handful of these methods – the rest (e.g., various creativity methods) will remain optional and student teams will select those that they perceive as the most fitting their needs. Therefore, while core methods will be present in requirements for individual stages of the project and will be part of the lecturers' teaching, optional methods will be merely suggested to teams. We plan to create an online toolbox of these methods that will help students in the application. We intend to have this toolbox publicly available in the future through a dedicated website – not only for students but also for other people interested in innovations.

Besides that, we plan to give teams more responsibility for setting their deadlines for the project during the semester. Finally, we will consider having a final evaluation of projects (games) in a form of a small university fair during which students will present their games to attendees-other students who will evaluate them. In this scenario, it would be meaningful to set university students as a target group for the game.

The initiative provides ample room for continuous development. We plan to evaluate each iteration during the semester and after it and gradually adjust it to better reach the primary teaching goals – create new student innovators.

References

Barney, J., 1991. Firm resources and sustained competitive advantage. Journal of Management 17 (1), 99–120.

Kim, W.C., Mauborgne, R., 2015. Blue Ocean Strategy, Expanded Edition: How to Create Uncontested Market Space and Make the Competition Irrelevant. Harvard Business Review Press, Cambridge.

Cooper, R.G., 2017. Winning at New Products: Creating Value Through Innovation, 5th edition. ed. Basic Books, New York.

Goffin, K., Mitchell, R., 2016. Innovation Management: Effective Strategy and Implementation, 3rd ed. Red Globe Press, London.

Osterwalder, A., Pigneur, Y., 2010. Business Model Generation: A Handbook for Visionaries, Game Changers, and Challengers. Wiley, Hoboken.

Osterwalder, A., Pigneur, Y., Bernarda, G., Smith, A., 2015. Value Proposition Design: How to Create Products and Services Customers Want. Wiley, Hoboken.

Osterwalder, A., Pigneur, Y., Smith, A., Etiemble, F., 2020. The Invincible Company: How to Constantly Reinvent Your Organization with Inspiration From the World's Best Business Models. Wiley, Hoboken.

Author Biographies

Michal Jirásek is an assistant professor at Department of Corporate Economy at Faculty of Economics and Administration, Masaryk University, Czech Republic. His teaching and research focus on behavioral strategy, especially on performance feedback and decision making, innovation management and ethical issues in business decision making.

Eva Švandová is an assistant professor at Department of Corporate Economy at Faculty of Economics and Administration, Masaryk University, Czech Republic. Her teaching and research focus on innovation management and supply chain management.

Learning Innovation for Enterprise: Skills for the LIFE of an entrepreneurial student

Roisin Lyons[1], Catherine Faherty[2], Peter Robbins[2] and Philip O'Donnell[2]
[1]University of Limerick, Ireland
[2]Dublin City University, Ireland
roisin.lyons@ul.ie

1. Introduction

Learning Innovation for Enterprise (LIFE) is a year-long enterprise module taken by ~630 first-year students across eight undergraduate business programmes. It is designed to illustrate how innovation unfolds in key commercial, entrepreneurial and organisational contexts. In a team-taught and multi-modal environment, the module incorporates multiple layers of industry engagement, gamification, critical and creative thinking.

We designed and curated four separate, but meaningful sets of experiences for our students – formulated around our **BOSS** model shown in Figure 1.

Figure 1: The BOSS Model

The first element (**Big** Enterprise) brings students into contact with the world of the 'intrapreneur'. They meet with the Head of the Innovation Lab at Citibank and work in groups on a live innovation project aimed at developing new ideas around banking for millennials. To equip them for this task, we teach them the basics of design thinking and they use this process to develop their new concepts.

(**Own** Enterprise/ Entrepreneurship) requires students to participate in Startup Week in Dublin where they are asked to attend talks, seminars, workshops and events where they can learn about the entrepreneurial process. They then reflect on their experience in an online e-portfolio, synthesising the experience with their academic reading.

Small and Family Enterprise is the focus of the third element. Here, the students are introduced to the underlying dynamics and practices that undergird successful multi-generational family enterprises. We bring in guest speakers from long-standing family businesses across Ireland for live interactive case studies. For their project, we use a flipped classroom approach whereby students apply their new knowledge to real-world case studies, creating documentary-style videos and podcasts depicting innovation within family enterprises in their locality.

The fourth section is focused on **Social** Enterprise. Our five-day social innovation hackathon series ('DCU Hack4Change') requires students to focus on contemporary societal issues including climate change, mental health and wellbeing, and inclusivity, and then document their experiences in an e-Portfolio. Students are supported in formulating innovative solutions to specific dimensions of these problems by attending talks and receiving coaching from expert mentors including social entrepreneurs, charity leaders, political figures, activists, and academic staff. Across both formats (in person and virtual), student participants have consistently identified the hackathon as a highlight of their first-year academic experience.

Monday
March 9th
Mental Health and Wellbeing

Tuesday
March 10th
Fast Fashion

Wednesday
March 11th
Smarter Travel

Thursday
March 12th
Climate Action and Sustainability

Friday
March 13th
Inclusive Society

To date, the module has won several prestigious awards for its innovative approach to teaching and learning. These include: Winner of the 2021 European Consortium of Innovative Universities Team Award for Innovation in Teaching and Learning; Winner of AACSB's Business Education Alliance 2020 'Innovations That Inspire' award DCU President's Award for Excellence in Teaching & Learning in recognition of the teaching team's "exceptional, innovative, and transformational contribution to the student experience". The module also forms a best practice example in in the new course "Higher Education 4.0 – Certifying Your Future: https://www.futurelearn.com/courses/higher-education-certifying-your-future

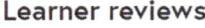

2. The learning outcomes

According to the DCU Teaching & Learning Strategy, the most valued 21st century graduates are those that can find effective and innovative solutions to new and complex challenges. The foundations of those solutions are academic excellence, an ability to work with others in developing new approaches to problems and communicating those solutions to relevant audiences. The Learning Outcomes were created in line with the module aims and in keeping with pedagogical best practices of lower order to higher order thinking, and skill development.

As such, we would like our students in the LIFE module to:

1. Engage with and reflect on enterprise-related content
2. Research the social, cultural and economic landscape to identify areas of innovation.
3. Apply idea generation techniques to solve enterprise challenges.
4. Discuss the main concepts and techniques relating to innovation and entrepreneurship.
5. Work collaboratively in teams to design and produce 'research-ready' innovation concepts in response to a client brief.

Our team is committed to fostering the development of these skills in our students and this commitment is reflected in the following ways:

Employability Skills: Our module is designed to ensure our students are equipped with the appropriate skills required to flourish in the workplace, whatever context in which they may find themselves. LIFE allows students to gain insight into the increasingly dynamic world of work across a range of organisational contexts, such as corporate enterprise, family business, entrepreneurship and the non-profit sector.

Providing a 21st Century Learning Experience: We utilised new digital technologies in the teaching and assessment of the module (e.g. the 'GatherTown' platform and the gamification elements). This use of technology-enhanced learning improved the learning experience of our students, ensuring flexibility in delivery and engagement.

Developing Entrepreneurial Skills in our Students: By providing opportunities for entrepreneurial experiential learning, our module fosters a spirit of innovation and promotes an entrepreneurial mind-set in our students. For example, as part of our focus on entrepreneurship, students were required to attend one of 90 free events at Startup Week. The five-day event brought over 3500 entrepreneurs, local leaders and friends together to build momentum and foster innovation around the city. Our students attended talks focused on entrepreneurship, UX design, scaling, investment and more, and reflected on their experience within their learning e-Portfolios.

Integrating Research Opportunities in our Undergraduate Degree Programmes: Our module is led by research active staff, ensuring the integration of cutting-edge research into our teaching activities. We partnered with established research centres, such as DCU National Centre for Family Business, to further raise student awareness of University research and engagement activities. In addition, the module assessment was designed to provide research-integrated learning experiences for our students by providing opportunities for them to develop their research skills. For example, as part of the "flipping the classroom" assignment, students conducted qualitative research by interviewing family business leaders across Ireland and applying the theories and frameworks learned in class to these real-life case studies.

As stated, the module is divided into four parts and each carries its own assessment, including both-team based and individual. Each of these elements contribute to students' overall grade at the end of the year.

Table 1: Assessment methods employed for each element

Elements	Assessment T	Which outcomes are measured	%
Start-Up OWN	E-Portfolio	A reflective individual journal that students use to document their experiences of external entrepreneurship events. Learning Outcomes: 1) Employability Skills and 3) Entrepreneurial Skills.	20
Corporate BIG	Digital Project	Students were divided into teams of 5-6 and we ran tutorials in smaller groups to teach them the tools and skills of design thinking. Their task was to develop a suite of ideas for the 'client' Citibank of new products/services or experiences for banking for Millenials. Learning Outcomes:	25

Elements	Assessment T	Which outcomes are measured	%
		1) Employability Skills and 3) Entrepreneurial Skills.	
SMALL/ Family	Digital Project	Students are required to work in teams of 5-6 and create a documentary-style video clip depicting innovation within a multigenerational family business in their locality. Learning Outcomes: 1) Employability Skills and 4) Research Opportunities.	25
SOCIAL	E-Portfolio	A reflective journal that students will use to document their experiences with a Social Innovation Hackathon (a 1 full-day event). The document will also be used to indicate participation in the hackathon and related lectures. Learning Outcomes: 1) Employability Skills, 2) 21st Century Learning Experience and 3) Entrepreneurial Skills.	20
All	Attendance and Participation	Attendance and engagement is measured at selected lectures, tutorials and external events.	10

3. The Infrastructure

The module was developed in line with recommendations from the EU EntreComp Framework and incorporates many of the intended competencies and recommendations into its design. The module coordinator is a researcher in the specific field of entrepreneurial education, and our team consulted with numerous external experts in devising the curriculum. As such, the module is intended to specifically develop enterprise self-efficacy in its first-year students.

"In developing the LIFE module, the team undertook detailed feasibility studies and benchmarking exercises to identify best practice internationally having either visited or reviewed programmes in Harvard, Kellogg, MIT, INSEAD, and IMD among

others. The module the team have created is truly world-class and provides our students in DCU with best in class education. The ability for undergraduate students to experience entrepreneurship in different contexts is truly exceptional and will be an invaluable tool as they progress in their careers." – Eric Clinton, Associate Professor in Entrepreneurship, DCU Business School.

Among the many distinguishing features of the LIFE module is the alignment of the four strands, with the human and technological infrastructure that supports the module. LIFE is co-delivered by 3-4 members of the Entrepreneurship faculty at Dublin City University, each of whom is a specialist in one of the four module strands. Allocating each domain to a specialist in that area ensures students are exposed to cutting-edge, evidence-based insights.

Successful delivery of a module on this scale (~630 first-year students across six undergraduate Business programmes) also requires extensive 'behind the scenes' support. Where possible, student queries are responded to by one of two assigned Teaching Assistants using a dedicated email account for the LIFE module.

The assistance of 6 teaching assistants was also used throughout the module to assist with grading and the provision of formative feedback after each assignment. To facilitate this, extensive training being given to all Teaching Assistants at multiple junctures. The teaching assistants were provided with a grading rubric, and an automated feedback script tool with a pre-determined series of feedback statements (50) to ensure customized feedback was provided to each individual student, yet was within a consistent line of messaging. Before the group began, they were asked to grade practice assignments and discuss their results with the module staff. During the process, the lecturer then assessed and monitored all staff grades and gave feedback on whether their grading needed to be adjusted. This process was found to be robust, and an excellent mechanism to train new staff members in an effective and rigorous manner.

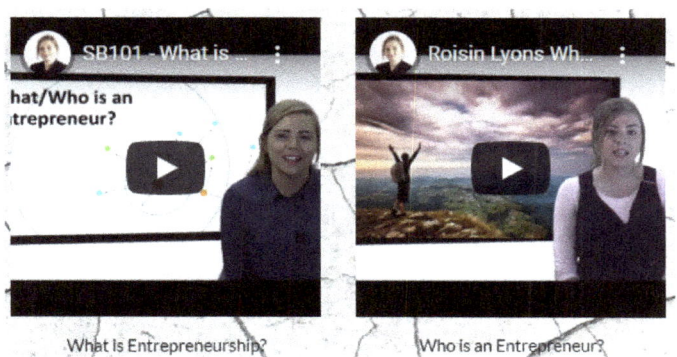

What Is Entrepreneurship? / Who is an Entrepreneur?

As the module was designed as a blended course from the outset, the module is taught with a mix of short Youtube primer videos (2 x 10mins each for each strand) to introduce the topic, a required reading list of 20 journal articles (5 within each strand), recorded podcast-style discussions about these selected articles to provide some context and assistance, annotated PDF guides for certain other of the selected articles. The module team require students only use these articles in their reflections and are not required to read beyond. It is considered in their first year, as they learn how to navigate scholarship and academic reading, this provides them time to engage with key texts more thoroughly. All of the artefacts noted above are provided on the Moodle ("Loop") Learning Management System within the University. Each aspect is gamified in that when students complete a task (e.g. watch a primer video) they are asked to answer a question related to it, and attain points on their profile as a result. These points ultimately become part of their attendance/participation mark at the end of the year.

4. The Challenges

In the academic year 2020/21, the cancellation of StartUp Week Dublin as a result of COVID-19 meant, in essence, that we were forced to create our own event which would provide for the students a similarly novel and hands-on experience. In conjunction with other universities, societies, and entrepreneurship stakeholders, we initiated StudentStartUpDay, a single-day event comprising a broad range of talks, workshops, and networking fora to ensure students could continue to experience the distinctively immersive and hands-on qualities of the module. In each case - where the engagement event was held in person and online - students wrote reflections on their experience, their observations and their conclusions.

In a similar vein, we were forced to transition our hackathon to an online environment. We hosted our first hackathon series in March 2020 and on the penultimate day, a national lockdown was announced with immediate effect, forcing us to provide alternative arrangements for those students that were scheduled to attend on the following day. While we managed to do so as an emergency measure (students were given the choice between attending a virtual hackathon that had been organised by a third-party organisation or attending a virtual mini-conference hosted by some of our Business School colleagues), we were confronted with the imperative of implementing an entirely different model for our hackathon in Year 2 (in 2021, when in-person events were not permitted). Here, we used the 'GatherTown' virtual platform. Many student participants identified this hackathon as a highlight of their first-year academic experience.

To pivot online for the 2020/21 academic year, we used the 'GatherTown' virtual platform to host a social innovation hackathon series, known as DCU *Hack4Change*. The platform combines aspects of gamification (each participant is represented on the platform by their own avatar, whose movements they control) and territoriality (unlike Zoom, GatherTown allows for participants to move freely between rooms, where they can interact with peers simply by coming into closer proximity to their peers' avatars), and which supports high levels of customizability so we could create a unique and engaging virtual space for students). In preparing for students to interact with the GatherTown platform, we ensured that we had the assistance of teaching assistants and digital staff, trained in how to navigate the platform.

Regarding the assessment throughout the Hackathon experience in 2021, the students were asked to complete a HackImpact Canvas (see below) which outlined their proposed idea. In line with this, they were asked to create a presentation and video of their proposed idea, to present to the judges on the final day of the event. In addition to the main prize there were additionally a number of special prizes as sponsored by key companies – such as the best video pitch.

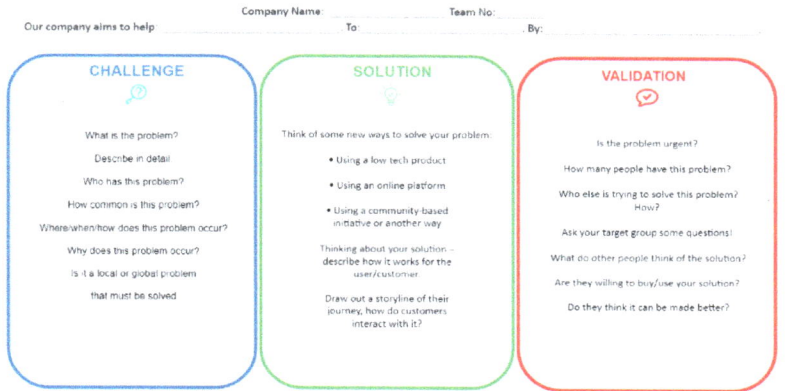

5. How the initiative was received

Students and student societies were heavily involved in the module planning process—voting on relevant topics and speakers to embed into the module and collaborating on events. For instance, four enterprise society groups were involved in the running/collaboration of the hackathon events. In addition, the module underwent an in-depth review at the conclusion of its first year, and held an open call for discussion over Zoom for feedback and new ideas for the hybrid approach of 2020/21. Student engagement is essential for high-quality learning and the delivery of the module is centred around active student participation and engagement. Below is a sample of quotations from our students regarding the LIFE module.

> "Personally, I have always had the impression that being an entrepreneur was somewhat impossible! I chose this event in the hope that it would challenge my initial perception of entrepreneurship and it's safe to say that this event really turned my doubts on their head! … I became so much more convinced of my ability to become an entrepreneur.

> "I didn't have much previous knowledge on Enterprise. I never took an interest as I didn't really understand it. Entrepreneurship was a foreign concept to me and my first proper encounter with the subject was in the SB101 (L.I.F.E) lecture. Before I just assumed that

all you needed was a very good idea if you wanted to thrive in the entrepreneurial sector. I thought entrepreneurs were mainly just creative people, who if they thought about a good enough idea, would just succeed. They were the lucky ones who found a secret to getting rich quickly and easily. ... Now after these recent experiences listening, reading and researching about entrepreneurship, my perception has changed. I didn't realize the depth of the role of an entrepreneur; the hours they put in and the sacrifices they make. There is more to an entrepreneur than just their idea. ... Overall, I now have a greater appreciation for entrepreneurs and their efforts."

"By attending this event, my thoughts about entrepreneurship have changed drastically. Before attending this Start-Up week event, I had a completely different mindset towards entrepreneurship and innovation. When I heard the word entrepreneurship, I immediately associated it with all things business and only those who hold a business degree. But now looking back, I realized I was completely wrong. By listening to both past and present DCU students from all five faculties, not just business, I have come to realize that you too can be an entrepreneur, no matter your background, degree or experiences. I have gained so much knowledge about entrepreneurship and innovation by attending this event and how simple it can be to create your own Start-Up."

"Prior to this hackathon I would have never pursued my own social enterprise as I would not know what to do and what steps I need to take, but what this hackathon has shown me is that it isn't something I should be intimidated by and anyone can do it. Once I apply my knowledge of Problem, Solution, Verification I believe I'll be able to develop my social enterprise to a point where I'd actually be willing to form a start-up."

A research study was carried out to assess the student perception of the hackathon and any improvements that could be made for future iterations in 2021. In total there were 285 responses to the survey sent out to the LIFE Module class, 277 of which were useful responses.

Item	Quote #1	Quote #2	Quote #3
26 who responded to the question pertaining to "Please suggest ways that we can improve a hackathon like this in future" wanted more group work activities to get to know their peers better, especially after spending their first year of university online.	"Enjoyed working in groups and having to make new friends"	"More group elements - got to interact with issues more as talking to people instead of sitting in talks on your own."	"More than just one group dynamic to increase the amount of people you get to interact with"
37 respondents enjoyed the mentoring aspect of the Hackathon, but would have preferred having more time with their mentor	"Instead of having one mentoring session during the week, have maybe a couple shorter ones throughout the week so to help guide us through the process and run ideas by."	"I think that having a few more mentoring sessions to help guide students through the Hackathon would be very beneficial."	
25 respondents enjoyed the hackathon event but mentioned that they wanted a longer time frame to work on their ideas and interact with their group mates.	"Set up more activities in the evenings or during the day in which students could attend with their peers___"	"Everything was great, maybe more than a week next time."	"**Note: multiple evening events were organised including a live gig in the GatherTown bar, meditation sessions and a virtual table quiz.
30 respondents enjoyed the keynote speaker aspect of the hackathon, but expressed that they would have liked to have seen more guest speakers talking about a wider range of topics.	"I think the Hackathon was very educational and to have an even wider range of speakers would be fantastic."	"The Talks were brilliant, the opportunity to work with groups from other classes was great too. Wonderful to see an alternative approach to the working world of being a brick in the wall and promoting core values.	"I'd say if there could be speakers from other countries too, it would give a deeper perspective on issues."
22 respondents mentioned in their survey that the aspect that they appreciated the most was the staff effort that was executed to make the hackathon happen the way it did	"The amount of effort put into this hackathon was exceptional. I think every student appreciated the work and time that was dedicated to this. Thank you for the experience."	"The Organizers did really well to achieve what they did, given the limitations of lockdown and zoom. It will never be as good as an in-person hackathon but I was impressed with their efforts.	"Very enjoyable experience, appreciate the great deal of effort the college and staff went through to organise the event"
17 of those who responded to the question pertaining to 'Anything else you wish to share about your hackathon experience' felt they had a greater knowledge of social entrepreneurship and innovation following the hackathon than they did beforehand, with many saying that they now would aspire to become a social entrepreneur	"I enjoyed this hackathon, it was different from any other experience before. I was able to learn as well as have fun." "Opened up my eyes to the world of social innovation and demonstrated to me that a career in social innovation isn't as out of reach as I had previously thought"	"I absolutely loved the hackathon. This first year of college has been quite difficult so far and the hackathon was a comfortable and fun opportunity to learn new things and make friends at the same time" "It was a great experience. I'm hoping no future hackathon will be done remotely/online and I believe the one we were given was facilitated phenomenally."	"Highly enjoyed the hackathon. Professionally and efficiently hosted with warmth. Everyone was friendly and very helpful. It created a space to hash ideas out and create new ones. It broadened my horizon. I always saw myself contributing to charity as an entrepreneur but I had never thought of creating a social business which I am now excited about." Many thanks for a magical experience)"
24 who responded to the question pertaining to "Please suggest ways that we can improve a hackathon like this in future" wanted more interaction between participants.	"If possible, I think a combination of in person and online events would be better in appropriate circumstances."	"More interaction with people" "The live music was really good, maybe hold another night of it if possible?" "expand prize options"	The hackathon was very impressively organized. If it were to go ahead in the same format, I wouldn't change anything. Students themselves will be the ones who determine their success. If we all engage and interact even more, it would further improve a hackathon like this in the future."

Once the data had been fully screened, the open-ended questions were assessed by one of the research team, and grouped by the results of these themes and some corresponding quotes from students can be found below. These open-ended questions were optional items for students to complete. The quantitative analysis is part of a larger cross-university research project and will be analysed against multiple hackathon formats to provide empirical insights on the efficacy of such pedagogies on student engagement, student innovation and student perceptions of climate change and their university.

The work of our team has also been strongly supported by colleagues within our group, school and across the wider DCU community. To illustrate this, a sample of quotations from DCU colleagues is included below.

"The LIFE module provides a high-quality, innovative learning environment for our undergraduate students. This is an example of DCU's ongoing commitment to redesigning undergraduate student experience, mixing transversal skills and innovation and entrepreneurship skills together. The module incorporates developmental learning experiences for students through participation in enterprising activities such as Dublin Startup Week and DCU Hack4Change. These activities support our students in becoming enterprising, creative and solution-oriented individuals. The module combines in-class learning with industry engagement activities, collaborating with small-medium multigenerational family enterprises and large multinational enterprises. The team prioritises research-led teaching, providing significant benefits to student learning and development." – Eoghan Stack, Commercial Director, DCU Business School.

"I believe the LIFE module has been enormously successful in helping students to gain key entrepreneurial skills such as problem-solving, communication, risk-taking and teamwork. It has encouraged students to push boundaries, to think creatively and be confident enough in their own ability to take the risks necessary to succeed. Effective entrepreneurship education relies on both teachers and the culture of the institution to support. In particular, the teachers involved need a broad range of competencies to successfully embed entrepreneurial education into the curriculum and that is something the team have brought to this module." – Orla Feeney, Assistant Professor in Accounting, DCU Business School.

Don't just read about the outcome, see it for yourself!

To see a summary of the DCU Hack4Change event in 2020 (in a physical location) please see our video here: https://www.youtube.com/watch?v=sfI76dKSqIw

To see a summary of the DCU Hack4Change event in 2021 (online, on GatherTown) please see our video here: https://www.youtube.com/watch?v=fK-6FhTjo-q&t=11s

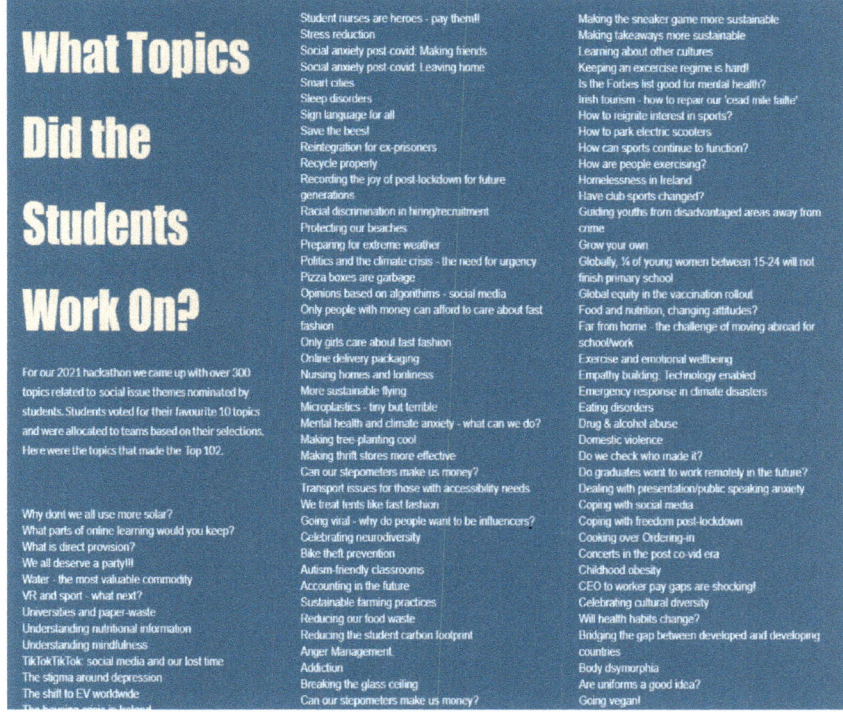

6. Plans to further develop the initiative

Developed from its inception as a hybrid module, integrating elements of video-based teaching, annotated articles and podcasts with live events, we aim to expand this further developing enhanced badging systems into our learning management system (LMS) platform ("Loop").

Own Enterprise
- Lecture content (Week 4)
- Tutorial content (Weeks 5/6)
- Online content (Weeks 4-7)

In developing the LIFE module, we undertook detailed feasibility studies and benchmarking exercises to identify best practice internationally, having either visited or reviewed programmes in Harvard, Babson, Kellogg, MIT, INSEAD, and IMD, among others. In addition, following delivery of the module, we undertook a 360-degree feedback process. We engaged in extensive stakeholder feedback which centered around both the student experience and feedback from our external partners—the start-up community, Citibank, and the family business sector. This benchmarking process has now been established and we intend to continue this, adding LIFE alumni into the group iteratively.

Much of the learnings from the module have been shared with the wider community and internally in DCU. In fact, a 70-page report was created documenting how the hackathon events (offline and online) were run; this is intended to be a useful pedagogical resource for other teachers in the field. Because LIFE was created as a blended module, incorporating live lectures, gamified engagement activities and asynchronous content videos, the module is particularly geared for hybrid delivery—a pivotal development for the post-covid teaching context of today.

An important and direct consequence of the success of LIFE has been the recent development of a follow-on module which will be delivered to all second years in DCU Business School.

Author biographies

Dr. Roisin Lyons holds a Ph.D. in Entrepreneurship Education and has taught innovation, entrepreneurship and social entrepreneurship to cohorts in Dublin and Saudi Arabia. She has recently joined the Kemmy Business School in the University of Limerick. Her research focuses on open-source innovation, entrepreneurial tendency development, and pedagogical design (hackathons, gamification, experiential activities for large-class contexts).

Dr. Catherine Faherty earned her PhD from DCU Business School in 2018, during which time she held visiting Research Fellow positions at Northwestern University USA and Northeastern University USA. Catherine's research focuses on trust dynamics in organizational contexts, specifically family-owned enterprises.

Dr. Peter Robbins is one of Ireland's foremost experts in innovation and former global head of innovation excellence for GlaxoSmithKline. Peter's PhD is in Innovation. His area of research is how firms organise for innovation. He is a former head of the Department of Design Innovation in Maynooth University.

Dr Philip O'Donnell was awarded his PhD by DCU Business School in 2020, his doctoral research focusing on entrepreneurship in resource-deprived settings. Much of his research centres on the Developing World, Africa in particular, and it covers topics such as livelihood strategies, economic informality, and social capital.

Design of a Regional Innovation Ecosystem

Vikram Singh Parmar[1], Neeraj Sonalkar[2], Ade Mabogunje[2], Prafull Anubhai[3], Larry J Leifer[2]

[1] Norwegian University of Science and Technology, Trondheim, Norway
[2] Center for Design Research, Stanford University, USA
[3] Ahmedabad University, Gujarat, India

vikram.s.parmar@ntnu.no

1. Introduction

A successful innovation ecosystem in a country could bring prosperity, generate employment opportunities, and increase cash flows. For building and sustaining such an innovation ecosystem, country would need bright citizens that are risk taking and willingly wants to become entrepreneurs. Inducing spirit of entrepreneurship in a socially complex context such as India needs questioning status-quo of existing social norms, safe job mindset and developing community of people that would strive to make societal impact. The Ahmedabad University (AU) in India wanted to develop an innovation eco system in the western region of Gujarat that could later be scaled up at a national level. The university management firmly believed that India as a country has young individuals with high engineering knowledge, institutions that are globally known in engineering, design, and management, and individuals that could be trained to become entrepreneurs and venture capitalists.

The University management collaborated with high-net-worth individuals to provide endowment towards establishing VentureStudio (VS): design driven innovation centre. VS offered a six-month design fellowship program to coach venture fellows/entrepreneurs belonging to varied educational backgrounds, economic strata, and age groups. The VS also provides design and engineering coaching. VS curriculum design was based on Persuasive Education and Environment (PEE) Framework. The PEE Framework was formulated by combining design fundamentals together with well-known theory of planned behavior (Ajzen, 1991), persuasive technology (Fogg, 2003), and diffusion of innovation (Rogers, 1995). This curriculum focused on a multi-layered approach that included working on the existing mindset of venture fellows, introducing design fundamentals to identify compelling user needs, build skill set for developing low and high-fidelity prototypes, testing of value propositions in real setting, team building, persuade them to "think big approach" for pitching, and upscaling their ideas for product adoption. So far, seven batches have graduated from this six-month fellowship program. In the first five-year, n=49 design fellows participated in our fellowship program and n=24 ventures were founded.

Our objective was to understand how an ecosystem—a network of engineers, manufacturers, entrepreneurs, researchers, investors, legislators and the physical environments they operate in— that sustains innovation in high economic growth regions such as Silicon Valley can be designed and built in India. There is a large body of research that seeks to identify factors that contributed to the development of innovation ecosystems such as Silicon Valley or Israel (Castilla et al, 2000 & Avnimelech et al, 2008). However much of this research is based on historical analyses; the results as such cannot be transferred directly to context such as India with differing infrastructural capabilities and cultural norms (Neeraj et al, 2016).

With our PEE framework approach to innovation and entrepreneurship education, we were successfully able to build a regional ecosystem by (a) training venture fellows (human capital) via our fellowship program (b) creating venture financial support (finance capital) by attracting high net worth individuals, and (c) designing a physical environment (innovative environment) that is non-judgmental and offered freedom to experiment.

In conclusion, VS has resulted in creating ventures that have either sold their IP to a large company in Silicon Valley or been able to generate seed A or B funding successfully. Entrepreneurs from ventures that ceased to exist have moved to innovation environments or have joined other startups as a co-founder or as employees.

2. The infrastructure

The infrastructure involves refurbishing an old school building of 24,370 Square foot (2264 Square meter) into VentureStudio. This included a prototyping workshop for building quick prototypes and testing. There were three full time coaches with design and engineering background that taught in the six-month fellowship program. There were three support staff and many external experts that were engaged with the VS initiative. The first chairman of the Ahmedabad University actively participated in this initiative.

In terms of facilities computers, software's as needed, and library with latest reading material on Innovation and start-ups were made available to all the Venture Fellows (VF). The physical environment has open office design, where no place is fixed or allotted. VF could sit anywhere to work and have their group discussions.

3. The challenges

The given socio-complex environment of India poses many challenges as far as innovation ecosystem development is concerned. We could categories these challenges into (a) shaping entrepreneur mindsets towards entrepreneurship, (b) building physical environment that is encouraging and non-judgmental towards new ideas, (c) creating community of high-net-worth individuals to actively participate in the regional innovation ecosystem, (d) designing Venture Design Curriculum, and (e) securing financial support for operational expenses of VS.

The challenges a,b,c,d were addressed by carefully identifying the problems, relevant theories to build theoretical framework that could assist in mapping the growth of innovation ecosystem in future. Further, creating a body of knowledge about theory and practice to build ecosystem in the context of emerging markets. We had proposed a Persuasive Education and Environment (PEE) Framework that was implemented from the first cohort of Venture Fellows in VentureStudio. The description of PEE is given below:

Persuasive Education and Environment (PEE) Framework

The PEE Framework comprises three phases: exploratory research, creative design research, and evaluative research. Together, these phases allow for empirical validation of the design and development approach. See Figure 1.

Component A: Design Driven Framework

Exploratory Research: Most of our design fellows joined this fellowship program with no pre-conceived idea, it was important to guide their problem identification process. Few fellows, that came with pre-conceived ideas also had an opportunity to re-evaluate their problem space and explore if it does have enough challenge to keep them motivated in this entrepreneurial journey. Exploratory research involves the following investigations: (a) Identifying the target user group, user needs, user characteristics, and social norms.

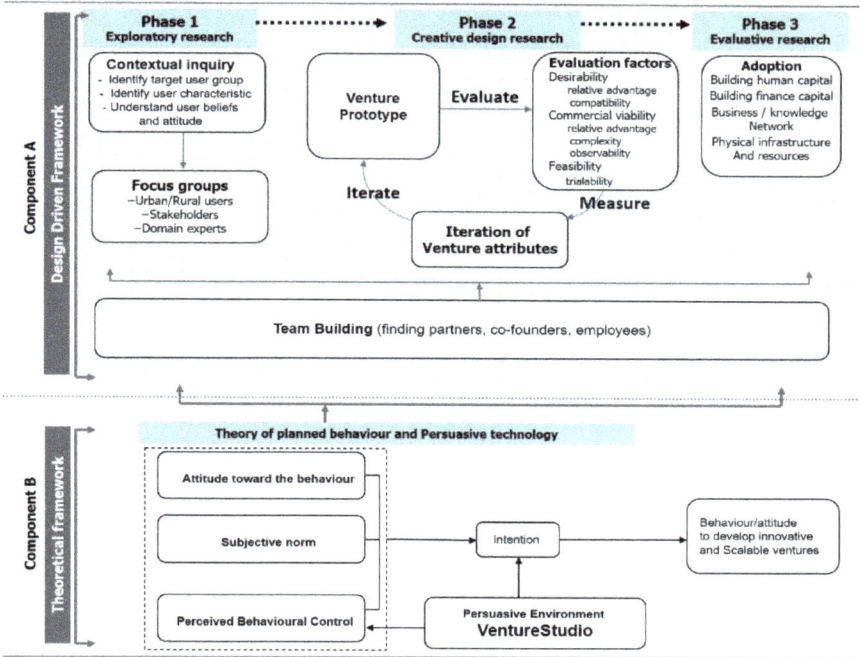

Figure. 1. Persuasive Education and Environment Framework

It also includes assessing the knowledge level of users (potential customers) related to problem that exist and perhaps needs a solution(s), (b) Obtaining insights about existing beliefs and attitude among users, relevant stakeholders about a selected problem that design fellows were committed to solve, (c) Formulating design brief for a new venture design, specifically the information content, form, and requirements for user interaction, (d) Identifying and outlining the responsibility of involved stakeholders in the design and development of a new venture design. This phase allows the design fellows and coaches to understand context and translate contextual factors into the design of products or services that meet the users' needs. These observation studies are mainly conducted in the field, along with actual users, stakeholders, government or non-government organizations, and stakeholders that could have direct or indirect influence in the development of a new venture.

Creative Design Research: This phase involves hands-on work to actually convert concepts into tangible solutions. This is often not a core strength design fellow have, however, their experience in this phase confronts them about their strength and weakness. Therefore, giving them feedback on which new skill they may have to acquire for overcoming their limitations. This phase involves the design, development, and iteration of different concepts via building Venture Prototype (VP). The VP enables individuals/teams to gain hands-on user experience and understand issues related to manufacturing, programming, or logistics. Additionally, it offers an opportunity to evaluate design strategies with their potential users from the initial design phase. This results in the development of a dynamic evaluating mechanism that can collect user feedback in a short design cycle, thus providing an opportunity for innovators to iterate VP design in line with user needs. To increase the rate of adoption, the user feedback is collected based on five product innovation attributes—relative advantage, compatibility, complexity, trialability, and observability—from the theory of diffusion. In the business term, these attributes could be understood as desirability (relative advantage, compatibility), commercial viability (relative advantage, complexity, observability), feasibility (trialability).

Evaluative Research: This phase involves measuring user adoption of VP by conducting short and long-term studies with users of VP. In this phase, the results from the studies are constantly integrated in the design of next version VP by comparing data collected in the exploratory research phase. This ensures that a venture idea is meeting the expectation of users and there is no mismatch in expectations. From an innovation ecosystem perspective, adoption of VS is evaluated in terms of how much human capital is trained, number of professional investors that are keen to invest and work as a core mentor with venture founders, degree of business and knowledge network created.

Component B: Theoretical Framework

This component explains the application of the theories that have been adapted to guide the design driven development cycle followed in component A. Three phases of the PEE framework have been supported by the theory of planned behavior, persuasive technology, and diffusion of innovation.

Exploratory research: In the exploratory stage, the Theory of Planned Behavior (TPB) has been adopted to understand social norms and perception of becoming an entrepreneur in the Indian context. The theory suggests that the combination of three variables—attitude toward the behavior, subjective norm, and perceived behavior control lead to the formation of a behavioral intention. These variables can be further understood as: (a) Attitude toward the behavior: can be understood as an individual's positive or negative evaluation of self-performance of the particular behavior. For example, in the case of entrepreneurship, this variable provides a guideline for investigating beliefs and attitude of individuals related to becoming an entrepreneur, how do they perceive entrepreneurial ventures, and perception about taking a risk to work on their dream ideas, (b) Subjective norm: is defined as an individual's perception of social normative pressures or other beliefs that he or she should or should not perform certain behavior. For example, this variable allows investigation into social beliefs that influence thinking of individuals to pursue a safer versus riskier career approach, (c) Perceived behavioral control: can be understood as an individual's perceived ease or difficulty with performing the behavior. For example, this variable provides guidelines for investigating the capacity of design fellows to question existing subjective norms and the ability to change their existing attitudes related to an entrepreneur and entrepreneurship.

Creative design research: The first aim is to design a prototype of a product or services and to test all value proposition assumptions with actual customers/users. In creative design research, we apply Persuasive Technology (PT). With a focus on persuading individuals to becoming an entrepreneur, functional triad framework from PT that illustrates the three roles computing technology can play: as a tool, a medium, and a social actor were adapted to design physical environment of VS, and curriculum that could shape DF mindsets. In the Indian context, the social actor approach is more effective because it offers a variety of social cues that elicit social responses from the design fellows. There are five types of social cues including physical, psychological, language, social dynamics, and social roles. In engineering entrepreneurship, all the cues were integrated for instance, (a) designing of physical spaces to push community or individual centric behavior, (b) designing and sharing content that could influence the psychology of design fellows, (c) using content and language that is widely understood by design fellows, (d) building teams that could spur constructive social dynamics, and (e) involving social role models to expose design fellows about venture narration, and entrepreneurship.

The second aim is to iterate the design of VP. User feedback is collected on the basis of five innovation attributes (relative advantage, compatibility, complexity, trialability and observability). The five innovation attributes were mapped in the venture design context and can be understood as: (a) Desirability (relative advantage, compatibility): idea of becoming an entrepreneur versus safe job should be judged by risk and scale of reward. In terms of venture, if offering has clear relative advantage over competitors, better economic value, and matching the demand of users would make idea desirable. The greater the perceived advantage, the higher the rate of adoption, (b) Commercial viability (relative advantage, complexity, observability): a commercial viability is based on factors such as price positioning in the market in relation to competitors, is customer base increasing after launch of venture, degree to which an innovation is perceived as complex to understand and use. How it will be marketed and made visible would increase observability of the venture, (c) Feasibility (trialability): feasibility of the venture is the degree to which an innovation may be tried and experimented with users in the context.

Evaluative research: In this phase, Desirability, Commercial viability, and Feasibility aid in evaluating the quality of venture design. The findings from this phase should measure the acceptance rate of new venture and act as an indicator for measuring user adoption. From the innovation ecosystem perspective, evaluation is conducted on hard and soft indicators. For instance, how many ventures were founded, how many design fellows were trained to become and think like entrepreneurs (human capital), how many investors believe in this vision and are keen to contribute as mentor (Finance capital).

Venture Design Curriculum: We framed the Venture Design curriculum for venture creation based on Schon's framework of reflective design practice (Schon, 1983). We applied eight key principles in the design of venture design curriculum. These eight principles informed both the structure of the curriculum over 6 months, as well as the type of activities, discussion sessions, and routines that we designed to constitute the fellowship program.

1. *Bias towards teamwork*: Teamwork is one of the key aspects of Design Thinking. Even in an entrepreneurial venture, the founding team is crucial to the success of the venture. The curriculum focused explicitly on innovating as a team, rather than an individual. Specific activities were planned for developing aware ness and skill in nurturing innovative team behaviors. In the book Psycho-Social Analysis of the Indian Mindset (Sinha, 2014) pointed out that Individually, Indians are brilliant and are likely to be very successful in favourable situations but may turn out to be counterproductive

collectively. To overcome such a mindset, various situations were created to let fellows understand and respect each other disciplines. For instance, engineering, commerce, design and management background fellows need to respect each other for the value they bring on table. Short- and long-term venture building exercise were used to explicitly discuss team conflicts, synergies, and work culture differences. We designed conflicts to confront design fellows and shape their mindsets about criticism and build attitude to receive feed-back constructively for improving the quality of their venture.

2. *Ventures are in service of a need*: This involves a focus on creating ventures that satisfy a critical need in society. The fellowship program was oriented towards user-centered venture creation rather than technology driven venture creation. In the initial phases of venture design, a lot of emphasis were given to phase of identifying compelling needs that DF would like to pursue and why? We believed, if a venture is addressing a compelling need of a society, it may have higher social impact and positively influence overall well-being of a targeted customers.

3. *Bias towards action*: This involves an emphasis on prototyping and testing. Following earlier studies that indicated a lack of prototyping orientation in resource-constrained environments, we paid particular attention to inculcating a bias towards prototyping and testing as a means of learning. Following the design thinking cycle this principle developed fellows understanding about customers, their needs, personas, insight building, design evaluation protocols, and building prototypes. Making design fellows perform short exercise that challenges their notion of impossible to possible. This included working on problem, concept, and building a physical prototype to test their assumptions. This process offered them insights about thinking in mind versus implementing their ideas in a physical form. Thereby reinforcing fellow's confidence to deal with any problem. How to tell a story that is convincing enough for investors to bet money on their ventures. Value of narrating an impactful story were taught via case studies including successful and failure cases.

4. *Fail early, fail often*: Having a bias to action in order to innovate demands being comfortable with failure. We emphasized understanding failure, one's response to failure and the skills

necessary to work with failure without fear. In VS, we made one dedicated physical wall to share failures. Anyone could write their experiences of failure including DF, coaches, and external experts, to communicate that any failure is a part of growth and learning, thus creating a non-judgmental environment across VentureStudio.

5. *Learning is key to innovating*: Learning has been linked to the ability to innovate in past studies. We emphasized that venture founders need to become active learners. Peer learning was encouraged through both formal and informal knowledge sharing in the community. For instance, design fellows had almost no experience of finance or investment design that includes know how to manage investors' money. Therefore, it was critical to develop basic understanding of finance and business modelling. Further, instil confidence among design fellows to take informed decisions about finance and business risks. Similarly, the design fellows were exposed to multiple skills in their fellowship program. They were prepared to acquire new skillsets if that is absolutely necessary for the growth of their venture.

6. *Innovating the self is necessary for innovating in the market*: We believe that in undergoing the process of innovation, the self-identity of the designer changes as much as the artifact being designed. This principle focuses on preparing founders to be mindful of their beliefs, values and the self-narrative and be open to changes as they are exposed to new situations in venture creation. It was important to develop individual capacity to be self- reflective. In the Indian context, opportunity to be reflective about own strength and weakness seldom exist (Sinha, 2014). Knowledge about individual self-awareness was achieved by focusing on fellows learning styles, personality, self-reporting of events, confronting them with conflicts and stressful situations. Simple exercise to write and share their honest reflections every day about incidents from yesterday with other fellows ended up building high degree of trust among design fellows, thereby making it easier to manage each other expectations.

7. *Exposure to multiple situations before commitment*: This principle emphasizes actively seeking alternatives before committing whole heartedly to one path of action. In the beginning phase, several external experts were invited to share possible opportunities that DF could worked on. Several videos depicting grit, passion, behaviour

pattern, or interesting philosophies were shared with DF, followed by reflective discussions to broaden their thinking and overall perspective towards themselves and developing entrepreneurial mindset.

8. *Beginning with the end in mind*: The curriculum was designed so that the fellows get a sense of how a process unfolds in time very early in the program through exposure to projects of different duration. All the DFs were constantly aware about the time factor and relevance to meet their deadline. Coaches in VS encouraged DF to set their deadlines and monitor if they meet them. This led to greater sense of responsibility among all the DF. As a process, DFs ensured that each phase of the venture design is completed to be able to access additional support from VS. The VS coaches didn't follow an open-ended design process that has no deadlines. Thus, offered timely opportunities to monitor progress of every venture.

The curriculum was structured into two stages:

(a) *Toe-dipping (orientation)*: In the Toe-dipping phase, the fellows were oriented to Design Thinking and venture creation activities in a period of five weeks. Following the principle of bias towards action, these five weeks emphasized experiential learning activities rather than lecture-based sessions. Also in order to encourage fellows to be active learners and to let them experience the end in the beginning of the program, we designed projects that enabled them to become familiarize with all aspects of the venture design process in a very short period of time. These projects, called as flash ventures started with user need-finding, progressed through concept generation, prototyping, market testing, business model design, and culminated with a venture pitch to investors. Our intention was to not give the fellows a curriculum where they passively wait to learn about business models in week 6 or financials in week 7. Rather we wanted them from day one to start practicing the process of venture creation from user need analysis to financial modelling. The first flash venture lasted for four hours, the second for three days, and the third for three weeks. Each flash venture enabled the fellows to iteratively practice the process of venture design at increasing levels of skill, complexity and understanding. Along with these three flash ventures, the Toe-dipping phase involved video case studies, improvisation activities, prototyping projects, teamwork exercises, business model case studies, and ecosystem mapping project. A daily routine of group reflection was introduced to give fellows and coaches, time to reflect together as a group on their past day's experiences, thoughts and feelings. The fellows maintained a journal to note their daily reflections. This activity was intended to enable the community as a whole to learn from each other, socialize, and develop openness to share feelings that were encountered in the process of designing their ventures. These reflections served as a data point on how the fellows were responding to the curriculum.

(b) *Deep-dive (venture development)*: In the Deep-dive phase, the fellows identified a venture domain, formed their founding teams and then followed the venture design process they had learned to identify user needs and market opportunity, prototype solutions, conduct market testing, and craft business and financial models for their ventures. At the end of the Deep-dive phase, they demonstrated a working solution and market traction. This led to subsequent registration and launch of their for-profit venture. The Deep-dive phase was less structured than the Toe-dipping phase. The coaches transitioned from a role of setting the activities to being available to the founders as and when required. Thus, there was a transition in control from the coaches to the fellows during the Deep-dive phase. The formal interactions between fellows and coaches were limited to weekly reviews and subject modules led mainly by practitioners from the surrounding ecosystem. Seed funding was made available to the fellows to cover their venture design and prototyping expenses during the Deep-dive phase. The group reflection activity was carried forward by the fellows.

Throughout the process, we were mindful of changing our curriculum post every design fellowship to ensure its viability in a context like India. Venture curriculum iteration was based on the following reflective framework. This framework enabled us to tweak our focus by regularly documenting design fellow's behviour, coach's response, and ecosystem stakeholder participation at the end of the six months design fellowship program. More details about the venture design curriculum can be found in other publication (Neeraj et al, 2016). As an example, we are sharing our feedback from fellowship 6:

Curriculum & Framing	Moving	Situation back-talk	Reflecting
Fellowship 6: Following the reflection from fellowship 5, fellowship 6 was framed more as skill building and execution rather than as mindset transformation	Fellowship 6 was implemented at VentureStudio from June to November 2014. A total of 8 entrepreneurs participated and at the end of the program, 3 ventures were launched. A few changes were implemented in the Venture Design curriculum based on the lessons learned from fellowship 5. The shorter 3-day flash venture was dropped in favour of extending the 3-week venture to a 5-week venture with a greater time spent on building Design Thinking skills. The coaches perceived that while the Toedipping phase helped develop energy and creative self-efficacy, the actual performance of teams in terms of user need analysis, concept generation, and prototyping was weak.	The performance of the fellows as the program unfolded did not indicate that the changes in the curriculum were effective in improving the performance of founding teams. The challenges that inhibited the teams' performance in fellowship 6 were more to do with lack of clarity regarding venture domain, coupled with team dynamics, and disagreement with coaches. The local coaches often evaluated the venture domain suggested by the fellows in terms of their own experience and at times actively discouraged fellows from pursuing ventures in domains they did not personally, see potential. The fellows did not always share the coaches' assessment, and felt inhibited in pursuing their vision. The fellows also perceived that the coaches were reluctant to release funds for prototyping or hiring services until they were convinced. This dampened the fellows' energy as they now felt they needed to justify every action to the coaches, who were now perceived more like reviewers rather than facilitators. This led to misunderstandings and	In the fellowships conducted so far, the Toe-dipping phase, which was an intensive introduction to Design Thinking was generally well-received with fellows participating actively in the activities and the daily reflections. The Deep-dive phase when the fellows starting to work on their ventures surfaced challenges in team dynamics, and relationship with coaches. Fellowship 5 followed a similar pattern. The negative dynamics with coaches was troubling and we realized the need to address this in the next prototype.

Curriculum & Framing	Moving	Situation back-talk	Reflecting
		mistrust in the relationship between coaches and founders. At times the relationship worsened to the point of fellows leaving the fellowship program. At times, the coaches themselves suggested fellows to leave the program if they were unwilling to follow the venture design process.	

Securing funding: The first chairman of the Ahmedabad University had managed to convince a group of High Net-Worth Individuals (HNWI) to give endowment funds to cover costs of operations and construction of physical environment for the VentureStudio.

4. How the initiative was received by the users or participants

The VS initiative was well received by all the stakeholders including entrepreneurs, business network, and government organizations involved in start-up initiatives. This was reflected in the increasing number of applicants for the VS fellowship program.

5. The learning outcomes

VentureStudio offering	How it is offered	Measurable result
Venture Design curriculum	Offered by design, engineering, and management experts for six-month duration	Curriculum attracted design fellows from varied education and economic background. Every six months, average 3-4 start-ups were founded. Grooming of venture fellows to become reflective and innovative in their approach
Seed funding for venture exploration	All the venture fellows were offered a seed funding support	Available seed funds were used to demonstrate their venture value propositions via working prototypes. Prototypes supported venture fellows in the pitching process.
Access to regional industry network	University management and	Contact with industry network and their owners led to formation of

VentureStudio offering	How it is offered	Measurable result
	mentors' network was accessible for in-depth venture discussion	Angel fund that could invest on VentureStudio ventures and other start-ups from the regional eco-system.
Workshop facilities for prototyping	Access to tools and machine for building low and high-fidelity prototypes	Workable prototype brought credibility to venture fellows pitch and confidence among investors
Physical environment for experimentation	Physical environment that encourages venture fellow to be experimental, and offers freedom to express themselves	Bringing like-minded people under the same roof led to venture team formation. Physical environment offered freedom to argue and deal with conflicts. Physical environment that delayed judgement, instead promoted radical thinking.
Disbursing government seed fund to start-ups in Indian Ecosystem	After carefully judging the submitted ideas and verbal pitching to formal committee members, VS had formed its own due diligence process.	The fact that VS was already involved in offering seed funds to its own start-up, Indian government initiative focussing on promoting entrepreneurship trusted VS to manage and disburse their large fund after due diligence. Thereby bringing additional credibility to VS initiative.

6. Plans to further develop the initiative

The implementation of PEE framework led to few successful start-ups from a first batch onwards. However, exact contribution to build an innovation ecosystem would require a bit longer observation to see how companies from VS will grow and influence the surrounding context. Theoretical linking generated scientific knowledge required to give direction to build effective Innovation and Entrepreneurial institutions, that is often over-looked in the existing approaches of innovation ecosystem development. In future, we will continue to observe the long-term impact of VentureStudio and evaluate if PEE framework really shortened the cycle of developing innovation ecosystem in a socially complex context like India.

References

Ajzen, I (1991) The Theory of Planned Behaviour: Organisational Behviour and Human Decision Processes 50(2): 179-211

D. A. Schon (1983) The reflective practitioner: How professionals think in action, Basic books.

E. J. Castilla et al (2000) Social networks in Silicon Valley, The Silicon Valley edge: A habitat for innovation and entrepreneurship, pp. 218–247.

Fogg, B. J (2003) Persuasive Technology: Using Computers to Change What We Think and Do. San Francisco, Morgan Kaufmann Publishers.

Avnimelech, G., Schwartz, D and Teubal, M. (2008) Venture capital emergence and startup-intensive high-tech cluster development: Evidence from Israel, Handbook of Research on Innovation and Clusters: Cases and Policies, 2, p. 124

Sonalkar, N., Mabogunje, A., and Leifer, L. (2016) "Developing a Design Thinking Curriculum for Venture Creation in Resource- Constrained Environment", International Journal of Engineering Education, Vol 32 No.3, pp 1372-1384.

Rogers, E. M (1995) Diffusion of Innovations. The Free Press, New York.

Jai B.P. Sinha (2014) Psycho-Social Analysis of the Indian Mindset. New Delhi: Springer, ISBN 97881-322-1803-6

Author Biographies

Dr. Vikram Singh Parmar is an Innovation Leader at the Faculty of Medicine and Health of Norwegian University of Science and Technology. He was involved in the institution building process of VentureStudio as a founding Director. Currently, he is responsible for creating an innovation culture with NTNU and convert high impact research into commercially viable ventures.

Dr. Neeraj Sonalkar is an Executive Director of the Human Innovation Design Lab and Senior research scientist at the Center for Design Research at Stanford University. He was involved as a joint- Director in VentureStudio. His specialty is to discern the right inputs needed by a venture, bring in the right people or tools to assist the founder, and guide the venture to peak performance.

Dr. Ade Mabogunje is a Senior Research Scientist at the Center for Design Research in the School of Engineering at Stanford. He conducts research on the design thinking process with a view to instrumenting and measuring the process and giving feedback to design thinking teams on ways to improve their performance. He was involved as a coach in VentureStudio.

Mr. Prafull Anubhai is an educationist besides being a Corporate Advisor. He is a member of the Governing Council of Ahmedabad Education Society (AES) and was also the first Chairman, Board of Management, Ahmedabad University. He was instrumental in securing the infrastructural and operational endowment funds to set up VentureStudio within Ahmedabad University.

Dr. Larry Leifer is a Professor in the Department of Mechanical Engineering at Stanford University. He is also the director of the Center for Design Research. His engineering design thinking research is focused on instrumenting design teams to understand, support, and improve design practice and theory. He was involved as a coach in VentureStudio.

The Youth Entrepreneurship Summer Program of the Athens University of Economics and Business

Katerina Pramatari[1], Angeliki Karagiannaki[1], Vasiliki Koniakou[2] and Vasiliki Chronaki[1]
[1]Athens University of Economics and Business, Greece
[2]University of Turku, Finland
 k.pramatari@aueb.gr; akaragianaki@aueb.gr; vaskon@utu.fi;
vxronaki@aueb.gr

Abstract: The Youth Entrepreneurship Summer (YES) Program is an annual two-week summer school focused on entrepreneurship and innovation, organized by the Athens Center for Entrepreneurship and Innovation (ACEin), of the Athens University of Economics and Business (AUEB). It is endorsed by the Greek Ministry of Education and hosted in the premises of AUEB, offering the participants a glimpse of academic life. YES primarily aims to promote youthful innovation and entrepreneurship, providing essential entrepreneurship and innovation-related knowledge and skills. Building upon young people's creativity and enthusiasm, it strives to train high school students into a new and disruptive way of thinking. It is based on an original methodology, theory, and practice, tested and further advanced through empirical research. The curriculum includes, inter alia, lessons by academic lecturers, analysis of case studies drawn from Greek and international examples, participation in business games, group activities, as well as processing and developing of business plans. At each stage, the methodology combines theoretical insights with actual practical experience, often in a gamified way, combing the elevated understanding of the relevant sector with the vital skills, appropriate attitudes, practical proficiencies and values an aspiring entrepreneur should have. During the Program, the participants work in teams to develop their business idea and draft business plans, the best of which gets awarded in the finals. Regardless the field of study they may choose, participation enhances students' understanding of the business world, introduces them to entrepreneurial way of thinking, and allows them to explore their potentials as future business executives and entrepreneurs. They also get the opportunity to discover the professional prospects in some of the most dynamically growing branches of the economy, obtaining valuable insights of the market and business developments. So far, more than 600 students from 240 high schools from all over Greece have participated.

1. Introduction

Research indicates that entrepreneurship is not yet a viable career path for the majority of youths, especially in the EU, but just for those equipped with the right skills, attitudes and values.

Having that in mind, all around Europe the development of youth entrepreneurship has become a key priority.

> "Entrepreneurship is too important to be left to entrepreneurs alone. We need to develop an entrepreneurial mindset in all young Europeans." - Johan H. Andresen

The Youth Entrepreneurship Summer (YES) Program is an annual two-week summer school focused on entrepreneurship and innovation, organized by the Athens Center for Entrepreneurship and Innovation (ACEin), of the Athens University of Economics and Business (AUEB). It is endorsed by the Greek Ministry of Education and hosted in the premises of AUEB, offering the participants a glimpse of academic life. YES is intended for high school students interested in receiving expert training and real-life market experience on how to create and develop their own business. It primarily aims to promote youthful innovation and entrepreneurship, providing essential entrepreneurship and innovation-related knowledge and skills. Its main objective is to introduce young people to entrepreneurship, assisting the participants to build their entrepreneurial skills, competences and values, and develop an entrepreneurial mindset. It is premised on an original methodology, theory and practice, that is further informed by the experience and data accumulated by ACEin. Up until today, more than six hundred students from two hundred and sixty schools from all over Greece have participated (65% from within Attica and 35% outside Attica).

Regardless of their future field of studies, the participants gain a more thorough and detailed understanding of the business world and the market needs. Moreover, they are offered the opportunity to explore their entrepreneurial potentials and understand the professional prospects available to them in some of the most dynamically growing branches of the economy. Moreover, they have the chance to obtain input from many successful entrepreneurs, pioneering and influential professionals, who share their experiences and visions for the future of entrepreneurship, innovation and economy. By the end of the Program, along with a memorable experience, all participants are equipped with crucial knowledge and skills that widen their academic and professional possibilities.

The curriculum includes, inter alia, lessons by academic lecturers of the AUEB, and distinguished market experts, analysis of case studies drawn from Greek and international examples, participation in business games, group activities, as well as processing and developing of business plans. At each stage, the methodology combines theoretical insights with actual practical experience, often in a gamified way, combing the elevated understanding of the relevant sector with the vital skills, appropriate attitudes, practical proficiencies and values an aspiring entrepreneur should have. During the Program, the participants work in teams to develop their business idea and draft business plans, the best of which gets awarded in the finals.

More specifically, YES has the following objectives:

Promote entrepreneurship from High School

The Program brings young people closer to the entrepreneurship world and teaches them how an idea, through work, can lead to a success story.

Change of mentality

The Program aims to alter the prominent way of thinking about entrepreneurship that tends to highlight the difficulties (e.g. lack of liquidity, inability to find partners, regulatory barriers, etc.), discouraging young people form trying to pursue their dreams. Instead, YES offers a new perspective towards entrepreneurship, and equips the participants with the necessary tools to overcome most of the obstacles inherent in entrepreneurship

Promote versatile team work, plurality and inclusiveness

YES aims to bring together adolescents from various places all over Greece, different schools, divergent socioeconomic backgrounds, with distinct interests and unique personalities. The participants are required to work together in teams, learning how to adopt different contexts and experiencing the benefits of plurality and team work.

Introduce young people to the Greek entrepreneurial ecosystem

YES aims to bridge the gap between young people and the market. To that end, each year entrepreneurs from all over Greece participate in the Program as lecturers, sharing valuable insights regarding the Greek business ecosystem.

2. The infrastructure

YES Program combines Human Resources; External Resources & Local Partnerships, and; Exams & Learning Methodology.

2.1 Human resources

The Organizing Committee

YES is organized under the scientific guidance of the ACEin Scientific Coordinator. Along with the Scientific Coordinator, the Organizing Committee, that is comprised of four to six individuals, are in charge of preparing the Program and ensuring that it will run seamlessly. The key duties of the Organizing Committee involve contacting and mobilizing all relevant stakeholders, disseminating the necessary information, and making all the arrangements required, including venues reservation, communication with the lecturers and the invited speakers, entry test preparation etc.

The Volunteers

Apart from the Organizing Committee, YES crucially depends on the enthusiasm of its volunteers. Each year the group of volunteers assists in safeguarding that everything will run smoothly. They are recruited through three distinct channels, namely an invitation through social media, University students' organizations, and the databases of previous years participants.

As a sign of gratitude, each volunteer is given a certificate of participation.

The Speakers /Lectures

An integral part of YES is the contribution of prestigious Lectures and Speakers, who share their experiences and insights with the participants. Based on their expertise, the Organizing Committee identifies and invites relevant speakers. The Organizing Committee approaches mostly entrepreneurship and innovation Professors, as well as distinguished Academics with entrepreneurial and/or business background; Startuppers, renown business people and entrepreneurs willing to share their success or failure story.

The Evaluation Committee

The Evaluation Committee consists of four to five Academics, tasked to evaluate and provide feedback to the teams during the Final Ceremony. Based on their decision, the three best teams/business ideas get to be awarded.

2.2 External Resources & Local Partnerships
Sponsors and Suppliers

Sponsors are entities or individuals providing scholarships or in-kind sponsorships. There is no limitation to the sponsorship each sponsor can provide. In-kind sponsorships may include food or miscellaneous supplies. Each sponsor is presented with their logo in the official page of the Program as well as in all communication and dissemination material. Moreover, sponsors may also choose to offer the opportunity of participation to up to five children of their employees.

Suppliers include food and miscellaneous contractors. For transparency reasons, they are chosen through an open competition. Quality, quantity, price and nutritional value are the criteria of choosing. Food suppliers provide breakfast and lunch every day of the Program, while miscellaneous suppliers provide notebooks, pens and other every-day needed items, as well as memorabilia of the summer school.

The State and High-Schools

Each year, the Greek Ministry of Education, Research and Religious Affairs distributes an official announcement to all high schools in the country, including all the necessary information about the Program. The letter is prepared by the Organizing Committee and the Scientific Coordinator of the Program.

Each high school is expected to inform its students about the Program, and assist the interested student to communicate with the Organizing Committee and apply.

Local Businesses

During the last week of the Program, a day trip called "Shadow of an entrepreneur" takes place. The participants are divided into teams of eight to ten and, escorted by the volunteers, visit businesses located around Athens. Through this day trip, participants gain a first-hand experience of how the working environment is, while getting the opportunity to see the facilities and get more insights and information about leading companies.

2.3 Exams and Learning Methodology

Each year an impressively huge number of applications is received. Unfortunately, it is impossible to host YES with more than sixty to eighty participants, as this would require resources that are not available. Hence, the entry test allows the Organizing Committee to evaluate the applicants and decide who will participate in the Program, based on their skills and competences. To ensure simultaneous participation of students from all over Greece, for reasons of equity, equality and transparency, a Google Form with an embedded timer is used. The test is aimed to verify applicants' skill level in Maths and English.

Lectures held throughout the Program aim at giving students a more in-depth knowledge of issues surrounding business and entrepreneurship. They are offered by university professors, business people, and researchers or PhD students with relevant research interest. They cover a wide range of areas such as finance, business, innovation, leadership, etc.

On the other hand, workshops cover two broad categories. Firstly, workshops, focusing on thinking and creativity, aim to help students familiarize with each other, and assist them to create ideas in a fun and quick way. The second category is the development-oriented workshops. Students learn to perform all necessary tasks in order to build-up their idea (e.g. financial analysis, market research, prototyping, UI-UX development, etc.).

During the Program's last stage, the participating teams pitch their ideas, and a group of experts evaluates their work as if it was a pitching event for disseminating their product and acquire investors.

3. The challenges

3.1 Annual Challenges

The Program's vision is to provide entrepreneurship and innovation training to all interested students, overcoming barriers related to the lottery of birth. Hence, systematic efforts are made for YES to be an open and inclusive Program that allows students from all over Greece with average, or below average family income, to participate and make the most out of this unique opportunity. Thus, participation expenses for ninety percent of the students are covered through sponsorships, while free accommodation for participants from the province at the University's student residence is provided.

Safety of all participants needs to be ensured as well. Volunteers' assistance is crucial to ensure that every participant will be safe throughout the Program, and their families will feel that their child is in good hands. Moreover, YES is open to participants with special needs. Thus, apart from training the volunteers to assist them, the venues are chosen carefully to ensure accessibility.

Finally, YES is organized after the end of the school year. Thus, whereas students may be genuinely interested in the Program they are physically and mentally tired after a demanding school year. Motivating them and keeping them interested is both necessary and challenging. This is why the schedule is drafted in a way that participants learn by doing instead of studying, and lectures are chosen carefully to inspire the participants and transfer their enthusiasm for entrepreneurship.

3.2 Unprecedented Challenges

A major challenge for the Program emerged in 2020 due to the COVID19 pandemic. The restrictive measures to prevent the further spread of the virus made it impossible to conduct the Program in person. Thus, an unprecedented dilemma emerged, of either postponing the Program or moving it online.

Finally, it was decided for the Program to be held online through the Microsoft Teams Platform. Shifting YES online raised serious considerations regarding its quality and effects. The overall duration had to be reduced to seven days, as several workshops and activities could not be held under the lockdown conditions. Teaching hours were reduced to six per day instead of seven, with larger breaks, taking into consideration the tedious effects online courses sometimes have on participants. Lectures content and duration was kept to the absolutely necessary while trying to pass on crucial knowledge and know-how as well as give participants time to work in their groups and receive feedback.

Thankfully, regardless to our concerns, the Program was once again a great success and managed to successfully fulfil its objectives. Friendships and personal relationships were formed, interesting business ideas were created and presented in the finals, and overall, partakers were left with a beautiful experience. How successful the Program actually was is best reflected through the words of participants presented in the section below.

4. How the initiative was received by the users or participants

Each year, participants are asked to give feedback regarding their experience. So far, participants seem more than satisfied with it, while some choose to keep in touch with the Organizing Committee, or even become volunteers. During 2020, a team of past participants decided to form the YES Alumni to enable all participants to keep in touch, exchanging experiences and help each other when needed.

Below we present some indicative comments.

> *"The summer school experience was unique through the people who framed it. The willingness and desire of the volunteers / organizers to stay with us, and take care of us even after 9+ hours of continuous work and responsibility was the behaviour of young people with vision and real interest. Thank you very much for YES 2018."*
>
> *"It is impossible for me to think of a single positive experience from this program. Friendships, excitement, emotions, vision for the future, tears of joy, and the most productive stress I have ever experienced. Accompanied by people with experience and dreams for a better tomorrow, YES will be unforgettable." – YES 2020*
>
> *"During YES 2020 I met new people from different places. Although we did not meet in person I feel like I know them very well as we spent many hours together trying to develop our business idea. I had a great time these days." – YES 2020*

5. The learning outcomes

YES, essentially constitutes an extra-curricular activity organized by a Higher Education Institution. Participants are trained in team-work with people that they do not previously know, and who may come from completely different backgrounds, learning through experience on how to manage such relationships to get the best possible outcome.

Participants seem to really change their mindset and mentality about entrepreneurship. They seem to be mostly affected by the stories of startuppers and industry/market representatives. It is also remarkable that several teams during the eleven years of the Program, turned into real business teams that continued working together after the Program, engaging in venture creation.

Overall, several criteria are measured to evaluate and ensure the highest final quality and outcome. Some are presented in total numbers in the Table below.

Evaluation Criteria	Outcomes
Business ideas generated	≥ 100
Lectures and workshops	≥ 250
Consulting and mentoring sessions	≥ 200
Scholarships given by private organizations	≥ 500
Volunteers involved	≥ 50
Professors involved (lectures, workshops, mentoring and consulting services)	≥ 10
Greek enterprises welcoming students for the "Shadow of an entrepreneur" day-trip	≥ 30

6. Plans to further develop the initiative

YES is more than an annual event, both for the Organizing Committee and for the involved institutions. In fact, it is an ongoing process that advances and develops with entrepreneurship, following the shifts and developments of the ecosystem. As entrepreneurism is a dynamically changing and evolving sector, one needs to keep an eye on the continuously changing entrepreneurial world and adjusting the program and its contents, to ensure that the program will continue having such a positive impact and will remain a beneficial learning process for the participants.

Moreover, education and teaching evolve, and new ways of teaching emerge. Additionally, the ubiquitous presence of technology and its penetration in teaching methods requires adopting new means and teaching modules.

Annexes

1. https://yes.aueb.gr/
2. https://management.aueb.gr/
3. https://www.aueb.gr/
4. Eurofound: Youth entrepreneurship in Europe: Values, attitudes, policies
5. Ferd's List: Europe's young entrepreneurs stand out from the crowd

Author Biographies

Katerina Pramatari is an Associate Professor of the Department of Management Science and Technology AUEB, Scientific Coordinator of ACEin, ELTRUN-SCORE research group and Uni.Fund Partner. She has received various academic distinctions and scholarships and has published more than 100 papers in scientific journals, peer-reviewed academic conferences and book chapters.

Dr. Angeliki Karagiannaki is a part-time lecturer at the Departments of Management Science and Technology, and Informatics of AUEB. She is the Managing Director of ACEin. She holds a PhD on "RFID-enabled Supply Chain Process Redesign using Simulation". Her research interests lie mostly in innovation and entrepreneurship and ICT entrepreneurship.

Vasiliki Koniakou holds a B.Sc. in Law from the National Kapodestrian University of Athens. She has a master's degree on International, European and Comparative Law, from the University of Turku where she is also a PhD Candidate focusing on Internet Governance. Her research interests lie in Internet and Technology Governance.

Vasiliki Chronaki is a PhD candidate at AUEB and Communications Officer at ACEin. Her research interests concern entrepreneurship and innovation, entrepreneurial competencies, mindsets and actions. She holds a B.Sc. in Financial Management and Engineering from the University of the Aegean and an M.Sc. in Management Science and Technology from AUEB.

Start-up Lab: An Innovative Entrepreneurship Education Program promoting Students' Start-ups

Alessandra Scroccaro and Alessandro Rossi
University of Trento, Trento, Italy

alessandra.scroccaro@unitn.it
alessandro.rossi@unitn.it

1. Introduction

The University of Trento Start-up Lab is an extracurricular 3-month program focused on generating business ideas, aimed at developing entrepreneurial skills and facilitating new venture creation. The program, since 2013 promotes entrepreneurship, creativity, and innovation skills for Master, PhD and postdoc students willing to apprentice entrepreneurial and intrapreneurial skills and to put the basis for a startup.

Start-up Lab is meant to complement students' curricula by employing teaching methods based on laboratory learning, problem-based learning, and challenge-based learning (Nichols and Cator, 2008; Observatory Tecnológico of Educational de Monterrey, 2015).

The course introduces learners to the topic of business design, a methodology for designing truly innovative products and services desired by customers and economically sustainable, through an iterative and incremental methodology that allows students to test the main assumptions underlying the business model before launching the product in the market. Students are introduced to various techniques drawn from lean start-up, business modelling, design thinking and user-centric design practice, and they familiarize, through a hands-on approach, with techniques of business design largely developed by practitioners (Ries, 2011; Blank, 2013) that have been more recently also validated by academic studies (Gambardella et al, 2018).

Whether learners are interested to learn how to work on new projects within an existing business or organization, or they are keener on becoming an entrepreneur ready to start a start-up, the program helps them reduce the risks of launching the product on the market, by helping them develop entrepreneurial ideas that represent a truly innovative solution to a real, pressing, and urgent problem felt from a specific market segment of early adopters.

This course corresponds to 8 ECTS (European Credit Transfer System) and around 200 workload hours divided into 48 class hours and 152 teamwork hours.

By the end of the course, students learn how to work in a multidisciplinary team, how to develop an entrepreneurial approach to problems, acquire the necessary vocabulary, knowledge, and skills to develop a solution, to use design thinking, lean validation methodologies, business modelling techniques, financial modelling, cash flow analysis, project management and finally they learn how to communicate productively within the team and with different stakeholders.

There is a long-standing debate in the field of entrepreneurial education regarding the efficacy of entrepreneurial education programmes, which has highlighted the role of a large set of mediating variables, such as, among others, the type of training, individual, cultural, environmental factors. Despite the limits of such scholarly debate in pinpointing clear-cut evidence advising the design of such programmes, there is also some agreement on the moderating role of different training methodologies and specifications in fostering positive entrepreneurial attitudes and behaviour (Gibb, 2002; Fiet, 2001; Honig, 2004; Neck and Green, 2011). Hence, the design of Start-up Lab is informed by previous work which has highlighted that elective programmes (Karimi et al 2016), proactive and practically-oriented approaches (Piperopoulos and Dimov, 2015) and problem-based education (Campos et al, 2017) seem to be more effective in eliciting positive attitudes towards entrepreneurship in participants.

2. The infrastructure

2.1 Start-up Lab and the innovation ecosystem

Start-up Lab is organized by CLab Trento (Contamination Lab Trento), an academic educational programme and co-working facility funded by the Italian Ministry of University and Research (MIUR) in 2017 that aims to enable university students with different backgrounds to work on the development of their business ideas through entrepreneurial learning activities (Secundo et al, 2020). Cross-fertilization is a principle inspiring the organization of all interactions for the participants and takes place at different levels. Firstly, among students coming from different courses and departments, who have the unique opportunity to interact and work together, typically developing their entrepreneurial project in a semester-long stint engaging with peers having complementary backgrounds and interests. Secondly, among students and instructors from different departments and disciplines, where both parties need to figure out a common language and how to effectively understand each other. Thirdly, with local and international stakeholders (companies, start-ups, investors, experts, etc.) who are directly involved in the educational activities and interact with the students in various ways.

Start-up Lab activities are held in the CLab Trento co-working facility, which is hosted by the School of Innovation (a cross-departmental centre for innovation targeting mostly graduate students, but also open to bachelors, faculties, and alumni). The facility is managed in collaboration with Hub Innovazione Trentino (a foundation set up by the University with other local actors, namely two research centres - Fondazione Edmund Mach and Fondazione Bruno Kessler - and Trentino Sviluppo, the local development agency) that aims at promoting the results of research and innovation in the Trentino region and supporting the development of the local economy. The location is a stimulating environment designed to encourage entrepreneurial approaches and to inspire the principles of proactive problem-solving, sustainability, innovation, and learning by doing.

CLab Trento is also involved in various EU-funded networks of collaboration and exchange with other Higher Education Institutions. Among them, a prominent one is represented by ECIU University, a European Consortium of Innovative Universities which brings together fourteen universities united by their marked international openness, quality, and innovation in teaching and research and the connection with the business world. The consortium aims to create a revolutionary and innovative educational model on a European scale, in which students, researchers, companies, public organizations, and citizens work together using the challenges-based learning methodology (Tecnologico de Monterrey, 2015) to find innovative solutions that have a positive and solid impact on society. In 2019 CLab Trento was awarded the Special Highly Recommended Award for Innovation in Teaching and Learning by the ECIU Consortium.

Start-up Lab provides students with the opportunity to engage with a wide network of instructors, staff, external experts, and senior and junior mentors. Senior mentors are typically professionals working in startups, companies, or in the Trentino innovation ecosystem, with sizable experience in business development and a passion for "giving back" by coaching students. After the completion of the program, senior mentors can help and support students and teams by offering internship and networking opportunities. Junior mentors are alumni of the program, usually former participants who provide support activities to the ones currently engaged in the program. The establishment of such a peer mentoring program further the learning opportunities both for attending students and past ones, while also securing inter-generational ties between alumni of the program.

2.2 The Start-up Lab Program

As a hands-on laboratory, Start-up Lab follows typically a 5-step process (Figure 1).

Figure 1: The 5-step program of Start-up Lab – University of Trento

Step 1: Idea Generation

The first step of the program takes three weeks and is related to facilitating the generation of business ideas: in this phase students form their teams through role-playing and ice-breaking activities and by participating in facilitation sessions aimed at identifying the problem they want to solve using a customer-centric approach.

Teams are created by students autonomously but considering some constraints set up by instructors. Teams need to be composed of at least four and a maximum of six participants and they must be as diverse as possible, accounting for different nationalities, disciplinary backgrounds, and gender balance of their members.

In this phase, students are fostered to adopt a divergent mindset in reflecting on potential business opportunities, trying to identify the problem they want to solve, not the solution. To focus on the problem, they are introduced to the Value Proposition Canvas (Osterwalder et al, 2014) and they are fostered to start their analysis by identifying their customer profile through the analysis of pains and gains. Once completed this phase, they match the customer profile with products and services that could resolve the customer's pains.

Step 2: Validated Learning

The second step of the program is represented by the validation phase, which takes four weeks: teams use various techniques belonging to the Lean Startup approach (Ries, 2011) to validate both the problem part and the solution part of their business idea. They use the Javelin board (Owens and Fernandez, 2014), which is a practical tool that allows teams to validate their business idea by experimenting and evaluating the problem with customers' by gathering evidence supporting or disproving the most critical assumptions underlying their business idea. Through several iterations, they ideally improve their understanding of the fit between the problem and their target customer. In this step they are encouraged to engage directly with their potential customers to get first-hand feedback, using different techniques such as online or in-presence interviews and surveys, for the validation of the problem they want to solve, and by crafting Minimum Viable Products to collect feedback on their solution.

Step 3: Business Modelling

The third step of the program is represented by the business modelling phase, and it takes two weeks. Teams learn Business Modelling as a methodology designed to fully define the outline and to optimize their innovative business idea. This step is focused on refining the value proposition developed in the previous step by understanding properly how to create, deliver and capture value. Teams build the Business Model Canvas (Osterwalder and Pigneur, 2009) of their projects and are asked to reflect, with the same iterative approach used during the validation phase, on the value proposition, target customer segments, distribution channels, customer relationships, key partners, activities, and resources, and finally, the cost structure, and revenue streams.

Step 4: Financial Modelling

The fourth step of the program is about developing a basic financial plan, mostly through cash flow analysis: students learn the essentials of what an entrepreneur must know about the economics and financials of a company. In one week, teams focus on the design of the cash inflows and outflows related to the development and go-to-market of the business idea and how and where to get effective fundraising to solve liquidity issues needed to launch or to speed up the growth phase.

Step 5: Pitching

The fifth and final step of the program consists of preparing a final pitch of the business idea to a panel of judges: for two weeks students are introduced to public speaking and familiarize with the construction of an effective pitch deck, while also improving their verbal and non-verbal language skills, the use of voice, and images to effectively communicate their ideas to various stakeholders and to tune their speech to different audiences (e.g., sales vs. investor pitch). Teams train their speech skills and slide deck contents through a series of so-called "Pitch Clinics" where they are given various opportunities to test their pitch in sessions with different pitch experts. This represents a precious learning experience since they can iterate and finalize visuals, contents, storytelling, while also perfecting the speech delivery by incorporating different feedback into the final presentation.

2.3 The Start-up Lab program: an innovative way of teaching

The Start-up Lab programme is not only a learning laboratory for students. It is also a laboratory of educational innovation for instructors and staff. Each year the programme has been constantly redefined, based on the needs of the participants and the desire to innovate the way we learn and teach. This was the case also for last year's edition (2021), which saw the implementation of several adaptations and improvements in the design, execution and delivery of the programme contents.

First of all, we introduced the concept that course participants are no longer passive learners, but are the co-designers of their own entrepreneurial experience and that supervisors act as guides/coaches and experts rather than professors. This innovation in teaching was also driven by participation in the ECIU Consortium (see 1.2). Following this approach, everyone is a learner: in the Start-up Lab learners are not only the course participants but also the instructors, staff, mentors, and stakeholders involved in the programme. Everyone who has been involved in the programme has felt the rising of knowledge and the strengthening of skills and practices: instructors learn new ways of teaching, mentors learn how to better support and coach teams, staff refine tools and practices through which better manage lessons and requests from participants.

Since everyone is a unique person with specific learning needs and different ways of learning (Gardner, 1999), we have tried to overcome the standardised approach of teaching, learning, and assessment, to personalise the learning process (see section 5). As students feel responsible for their learning, they can partly choose the agenda, co-designing their own entrepreneurial experience, and instructors leave their traditional roles to become guides and coaches (Hammond and Collins, 1991; Ní Bheoláin et al., 2020). Professors get off their desks and embrace a hands-on approach to teaching innovation and entrepreneurship using flipped classroom techniques: short videos on the 5 steps of the Start-up Lab are assigned for review before the lesson. Class meetings start with guest speakers presentations or with project status advancement and participants are asked to actively contribute to the discussion. Teachers are no longer teachers and students become the experts on the topic. Knowledge is built up by the participants in a constructivist approach (Elliott et al., 2000): teams start with what they already know about the topic, then investigate through interviews, surveys, online polls, literature review, fieldwork, etc. Students are encouraged to follow the 5-step process and be as proactive as possible, in all steps, contacting people, validating problems and solutions, reflecting on their business model, building the financial plan, and executing their pitch.

Students are encouraged to speak up, give feedback, ask questions, be involved without fear, and be confident that they are not judged for what they say. These messages are the key to developing a psychological safety net in the classroom and letting the dialogue flow more smoothly. Everyone can make mistakes and failure is part of the journey and the learning process.

During the programme, participants discuss with each other and with the mentor the specific topics of any given session and immediately apply those concepts to their project by working in teams and discussing their progress together with instructors, mentors, and also in group sessions with other teams. Co-operative and proactive teamwork is encouraged and stimulated by giving hints on the use of online collaborative tools and platforms. However, teams can manage their time and tasks independently. Individuals can evaluate their teammates and their teamwork through peer review (see section 5.4): this is a crucial moment for participants to communicate and clarify any doubts or divergent views. These are important turning points, after which teams may strengthen or collapse.

The quality of teaching is assessed at the end of the course through a student survey.

In Table 1 we compare a traditional model to deliver the classroom content with the one adopted in Start-up Lab.

Table 1: Main differences in teaching between traditional class and Start-up Lab

Traditional class	Start-up Lab
The syllabus as well as the learning goals are fixed and decided before the start of the course.	The syllabus is structured before the start of the course, but it can be changed in function of participants and teamwork needs. Learning goals are co-designed with participants (see paragraph 5).
Learning is based on passive assimilation and then repetition.	Learning is based on doing, interaction, negotiation. Participants start from what they already know and from their contacts.
Teacher-centered approach.	Student-centered approach.
Teachers are considered as knowledge holders and students as empty recipients to fill in (passive learning approach).	Teachers are facilitators and create a collaborative dialogue with students. Teachers support participants' course in building their own knowledge. Students are pushed into taking responsibility for their learning experience (active learning approach).
The role of the teacher is directive and holds all the authority.	The role of the instructor is interactive and shares authority with students. Usually there's a team of instructors, staff and mentors.
Teamwork is not expected: students work primarily alone (competitive value).	Individual work is banned: students work in teams (cooperative value) (see paragraph 2.1).
Mentorship is not included in the learning process.	Mentorship is one important pillar in learning: participants can exchange with junior mentors (alumni of the program) and senior mentors (professionals working in companies and start-ups) (see paragraph 2.1).
The assessment is decided by the teacher and usually is summative.	The assessment is partly decided by participants. It's a mixture of self-assessment and assessment made by instructors. The summative assessment is integrated with the formative one (see paragraph 5).
The teaching assessment, if required, it's standardized.	The teaching assessment is always included in the programme and it's provided to participants, at the end of the laboratory. Instructors, staff, and mentors can provide feedback to each other in order to improve practices.

3. The challenges faced moving the program online

Covid-19 restrictions have generated the perfect storm over traditional education worldwide at all levels, with striking effects in the case of laboratory and in-presence formats of learning, in entrepreneurship education (Ratten and Jones, 2020) and consequently in the Start-up Lab too. It has pushed further the full use of the emerging digital and smart technologies to cope with that new challenge (Secundo et Al. 2021). The pandemic situation has pushed further the full use of the emerging digital and smart technologies for

Start-up Lab: from the use of social networks and collaborative platforms (Gupta and Bharadwaj, 2013).

Through the 2020 and 2021 Editions, completely online, Start-up Lab discovered the importance of the use of technologies to increase an entrepreneurial mindset and entrepreneurship competencies (Smith and Paton, 2010).

In management practices, we have created digital spaces as hybrid learning environments that enable education in entrepreneurship and innovation. In addition, we had to rethink teamwork practices in a digital environment. Instead of working in the coworking spaces of CLab Trento, with tables, chairs, and flipcharts, teams, mentors, instructors, and experts were forced to collaborate remotely through online platforms. All formal and informal physical meetings took place via ZOOM calls: whether students were meeting experts or mentors, or doing team-building or informal meetings such as aperitifs, every activity was transposed from presence to online.

Teamwork was mediated by Miro's dashboards and post-its: teams could use collaborative virtual whiteboards on which to brainstorm, build their ideas and create their canvas.

The entire classroom management was organised in the Trello platform, using a central desk for the general overview of the class, the schedule, the list, resources, and templates. At the same desk, they had a quick look at the team and individual assignments. Then, each team had a noticeboard where they could organise tasks and activities and upload the required deliverables, through an agile and Scrum approach to project management skills (Campbell, 2019).

There was heavy use of Google Suite for specific deliverables, surveys, and evaluation parts. Online tools were also used in the face-to-face editions, but most of the collaborative work was done on paper, posters, post-its, in a physical space where people could meet, groups could contaminate each other, insights could come in coffee breaks or while walking down the stairs of the building. With the virtual edition, the instructors felt a mixture of curiosity and anxiety about the results of the creativity and innovation processes, as well as the effective teamwork, and the unexpected commitment and efforts of the students.

Finally, we had to strengthen the network with the other entities of the Trentino start-up ecosystem. For this, we called in experts and senior mentors who are typically professionals working in startups, companies or in the Trentino innovation ecosystem, with extensive experience in business development and a passion to "give back" by working alongside the students. After completion of the programme, senior mentors can help and support students and teams by offering internship and networking opportunities.

In addition, we have included junior mentors who are alumni of the programme, usually former participants who provide support activities to those currently involved in the programme. Establishing such a peer mentoring programme enhances learning opportunities for both current and former students, while also ensuring intergenerational links between programme alumni.

Finally, we had to strengthen the network with the other entities of the Trentino Region Startups' ecosystem.

4. How the initiative was received

Since its inception, the program has involved over 1000 students, 60 mentors, and 50 companies, developing 170 startup projects and supporting the creation of 15 startups. Every year almost 200 participants apply to the program and around half of them are selected, according to a series of criteria, such as the personal motivation to get involved in an entrepreneurship education experience; previous experience or involvement in innovation, entrepreneurship, and technology experiences; personal expectations on the program and learning goals. Team applicants with an already well-developed business idea are given closer scrutiny during the selection process, but the program also accommodates the application of students without ideas.

The Start-up Lab program is research-driven, since it is rooted in a systems perspective of training assessment (Baldwin and Ford, 1988) and aims at mapping the transformative impact of the participation of the students in terms of changes in their entrepreneurial skills and motivation (Bacigalupo et al, 2016; Oosterbeek et al, 2010). Students participating in the program usually report high levels of satisfaction and in surveys, they explicitly described their experience as transformative for their entrepreneurial mindset, intent, awareness and more generally in terms of their soft skills (as attested by a survey run during the 2019 edition, which is summarized in Table 2).

Table 2: Various measures of enterprising competency measured in terms of self-confidence, entrepreneurial intent, entrepreneurial awareness, and envisioned work situation for the 2019 edition of Start-Up Lab (compared with Cooper & Lucas, 2006 and Lucas & Cooper, 2004).

	CL2006 Pre-program N=217	CL2006 Post-program N=217	SUL2019 Pre-program N=102	SUL2019 Post-program N=102	SUL2019			
A. Self-confidence (self-efficacy) in skills: Evaluate your current skill levels compared to your peers (e.g., your classmates)	Percent ranking their skill "Good" to "Excellent"				Response changes from pre- to post event survey and sign test			
					N	N increase	Total change	p-value
Design something novel and innovative	61.0%	81.7%	56.9%	79.4%	102	52	65	0,0000
Solve an unstructured problem	75.2%	88.6%	83.3%	93.1%	102	47	65	0,0001
Clearly describe a problem orally	67.9%	82.6%	70.6%	79.4%	102	42	65	0,0063
Clearly describe a problem in writing	67.7%	78.9%	69.6%	86.3%	102	43	62	0,0006
Ask probing questions that clarify facts	70.2%	87.2%	72.5%	88.2%	102	41	68	0,0341
Motivate others to work together	71.4%	84.4%	78.4%	82.4%	102	36	66	0,1945
Recognise a good business opportunity	72.0%	86.8%	65.7%	81.4%	102	52	72	0,0000
Understand what it takes to start your own business	41.0%	87.7%	53.9%	81.4%	102	58	74	0,0000
Start a successful business if you want	41.0%	82.2%	43.1%	66.7%	102	55	72	0,0000
Evaluate arguments and evidence so competing alternatives can be judged	73,1%*	92,3%*	79.4%	87.3%	102	43	69	0,0147
Apply an abstract idea or concept to a real problem or situation	48,1%*	81.5%*	78.4%	84.3%	102	45	66	0,0009
Develop several methods that might be used to solve an unstructured problem	53,8%*	69,2%*	66.7%	86.3%	102	56	73	0,0000
Work on collaborative projects as a member of a team	85,2%*	85,2%*	87.3%	87.3%	102	39	61	0,0102
Lead a group whose members disagree	37%*	63%*	69.6%	76.5%	102	42	71	0,0480
Put a detailed plan into action	59,3%*	74,1%*	77.5%	87.3%	102	44	69	0,0077
Deliver on a job you have agreed to do	89,9%*	92,6%*	88.2%	94.1%	102	33	61	0,2213
B. Envisioned work situations by Time Periods (Immediately, Within 5 years, 5 to 10 years, more than 10, or Never)	Percent seeing themselves in situation within 5 years				Response changes from pre- to post event survey and sign test			
					N	N increase†	Total change	p-value
In new venture (owned by others)	70.8% **	64.6%**	85.3%	81.4%	102	17	45	0,1352
As business owner (employing others)	27.6% **	27.6% **	26.5%	27.5%	102	25	59	0,7024
Self-employed (working for self)	29.2% **	41.7% **	36.3%	36.3%	102	28	58	0,5522
C. Entrepreneurial Intent. Evaluation of agreement with the following statements:	Percent answers "Agree Slightly" to "Agree Strongly"				Response changes from pre- to post event survey and sign test			
					N	N increase	Total change	p-value
If I see an opportunity to join a start-up company in the next few years, I'll take it	39.7%	56.2%	68.6%	65.7%	102	33	58	0,1185
The idea of high risk/high pay-off ventures appeals to me	37.0%	45.2%	47.1%	60.8%	102	41	70	0,0598
I often think about ideas and ways to start a business	54.4%	62.1%	57.8%	59.8%	102	27	58	0,6530
At least once I will have to take a chance and start my own company	59.8%	78.1%	65.7%	66.7%	102	26	52	0,4449
D. Entrepreneurial Awareness. Looking back at the last month, how often did these scenarios happen to you:	Percent answers "Often" or "Very Often"				Response changes from pre- to post event survey and sign test			
					N	N increase	Total change	p-value
You talked about an idea for starting a Company	28,6%*	39.3%*	39.2%	60.8%	102	54	69	0,0000
You pursued an idea for starting a company talking about it more than once	14.3%*	28.6%*	22.5%	51.0%	102	60	69	0,0000
You took steps (e.g., looked into markets or technology) to follow up on an idea	7.1%*	25.0%*	25.5%	53.9%	102	60	78	0,0000

* = CL (2004); N=28; post: after 6 months; Response rate at post-test, 50.9%   ** = CL (2004); N=55;
† Earlier for new venture, later for business owner or self-employed

5. The learning outcomes

Start-up Lab uses to assess students integrating the summative evaluation (the assessment of the learning goals' achievement at the end of the experience) with the formative one which permits monitoring the learning process during the experience.

For Start-up Lab 2021 Edition, we decided to include a self-directed learning approach which is one of the 21st Century skills and one of the most recommended capacities required by the job market. That is why in the Start-up Lab, we proposed some tools to enable students to elaborate some reflections on their progress and their team's work.

Table 3 shows the assessment tools we used for the 2021 Start-up Lab Edition, explaining which are formative or summative ones, to whom they are addressed, who are the evaluators, the goal of each tool, the period in which the tool was proposed to participants and the outcome.

Table 3: Assessment tools for 2021 Start-up Lab Edition

Tool	Type	Recipient	Evaluator	Goal	Period	Outcome
Learning Agreement	Formative	Student	Instructors	Co-design the learning process with students. Students can identify their learning goals and their strategies to achieve them	At the beginning of the Start-up Lab	Completed and signed agreement
Self-assessment	Formative	Student	Student	Students can assess their initial and final entrepreneurial skills	At the beginning and after the Start-up Lab	Online surveys
Learning diaries	Formative	Team	Instructors	Teams evaluate their teamwork	In the middle of the Start-up Lab	One-pager
Peer Evaluation	Formative	Student	Student	Individual students evaluate their teammates and discuss in team	In the middle of the Start-up Lab	Online surveys + Team discussions
Team Reports	Summative	Team	Instructors	Teams show their outcomes	In the middle of the Start-up Lab	One-pager
Final Project	Summative	Team	Jury	Teams present their final business idea	At the end of the Start-up Lab	Final pitch
Reflection Report	Formative	Student	Instructors	Students can evaluate if they achieved their learning goals and reflect about the experience	After the Start-up Lab	4-pages document

Team reports and Reflection reports, semi-final pitches, and class participation contributed to the final grade. To get the final credits students also needed to deliver all other ungraded items (learning contract, learning diaries, self-assessment).

5.1   The Learning Contract

The learning contract is an individual agreement negotiated between supervisors and students to ensure that certain activities are undertaken to achieve an identified learning objective (Knowles, 1986). It is completed and signed by students and instructors at the beginning of the Start-up Lab programme. Through the learning contract, students explore their willingness to learn and their self-directed learning skills. Students discover their learning objectives, how they will be assessed, and also identify their learning goal and choose how to assess their results.

5.2   The self-assessment

The self-assessment is a survey of students' beliefs and opinions towards various topics on innovation and entrepreneurship, such as entrepreneurial self-efficacy, awareness, intention and work situation, which is adapted from Cooper and Lucas (2004) and Lucas and Cooper (2006). In the 2021 edition of Start-up Lab, we have also included the GET2 test (Caird, 2013) which defines an entrepreneurial tendency as the tendency to initiate and manage projects - highly entrepreneurial people do this more often and are more innovative in their approach. This self-assessment test aims to give students an idea of their entrepreneurial potential and entrepreneurial skills such as a high need for achievement, a high need for autonomy, creative tendency, calculated risk-taking and an internal locus of control. The self-assessment was completed by the students at the beginning and at the end of the programme.

5.3   Learning diaries

Learning journals are complementary documents to the Teams Reports (subsection 4.6) that were introduced to assess the team's ability to reflect on the ongoing process. They are a one-pager for each team outcome: the Javelin Board, the Business Model Canvas and the Cash Flow. In the learning diaries the teams evaluate how they are working to answer these four questions: a) What went well (strengths of their teamwork)? b) What did they learn? c) What to improve (weaknesses of their teamwork)? d) What will they put into practice (strategies to improve actions for the next steps)?

5.4 Peer Evaluation

Peer evaluation is offered to teams in two rounds. This is a way in which students can give feedback to their teammates and vice versa, experiencing important turning points in their experience. Feedback covers a) regular attendance at team meetings, b) level of meaningful contribution to team discussions, c) completion of team tasks on time, d) quality of work, e) cooperative and supportive attitude, and 6) contribution to the success of the project. The results of the peer review are sent to the teams, anonymously and in aggregate, to stimulate further in-group discussions. Mentors may facilitate these exchanges.

5.5 The Reflection Report

The reflection report (Gibbs, 1988) guides students through a 6-step process aimed at learning from the experience they have just left behind and at giving them the opportunity to put things in order, identifying what went well and what did not go well, and planning their next actions. This individual report refers to the student's learning contract and is completed by the students at the end of the course.

5.6 Team Reports

The team reports assess the quality of the team's work for each macro stage of the process: the Value Proposition Canvas, the Javelin Board, the Business Model Canvas and the Cash Flow. For each of these outcomes, teams are asked to explain the process through which they created them by delivering a one-pager summarising the overall process and learning.

5.7 Final Project

Teams present their business idea in two phases. In the first, called "Semifinals", all teams present their final 4-minute pitch in front of the instructors and receive an evaluation on the overall proposed solution, the level of innovation, the execution of the business model plan, the quality of the presentation and the Q&A session. Teams that manage to demonstrate the validity of their idea move on to the second selection phase. Selected teams can show and convince a jury of experts and potential investors during the Demo Day, which is the last day of the programme, and are evaluated according to the same criteria mentioned above.

The teams are ranked by the demo jury according to the criteria used in the semi-finals, and the most deserving projects are rewarded with mobility funds to visit incubators, acceleration programmes, research institutes, or to participate in workshops, events and meetings in Italy, Europe and around the world. All participants who have attended 80% of the course receive grades, credits and a certificate of completion. Individual participants receive grades on project function (50%), Reflection Report (15%), Team Report quality (20%) and individual class participation (15%).

6. Plans to further develop the initiative

Start-up Lab is a program that fosters in participants the acquisition of career-changing enterprising skills, which seem to be particularly appreciated by students, even when, after completing the program, students do not continue developing their project, as it happens in many cases. The program benefits from being embedded in a dynamic local ecosystem focused on innovation, where public research institutions are connected and cooperate in the entrepreneurship education system. Trentino has earned the status of the "Italian Silicon Valley": with almost 200 innovative startups registered, this is the region with the highest density of innovative startups in Italy (MISE and ISTAT, 2018).

In the close future, we plan to improve the linkages for participants with the local ecosystem by increasing both networking and job market matchmaking and by supporting the most promising and innovative ideas so to enhance the probability of continuation of the projects, also considering the local opportunities offered by applying to various acceleration and incubation facilities in the local area, also thanks to the support of the above-mentioned partnership with Hub Innovazione Trentino

References

Bacigalupo, M., Kampylis, P., Punie, Y. and Van den Brande, G. (2016), *EntreComp: The entrepreneurship competence framework*. Luxembourg: Publication Office of the European Union.

Baldwin, T. T., & Ford, J. K. (1988), Transfer of training: A review and directions for future research. *Personnel Psychology*, 41(1), 63-105.

Blank, S. (2013). Why the lean start-up changes everything. Harvard business review, 91(5), 63-72.

Caird, S. (2013), General measure of Enterprising Tendency test. www.get2test.net.

Campbell, A. (2019), Agile Project Management with Scrum: Secret Scrum, Independently published.

Campos, F., Frese, M., Goldstein, M., Iacovone, L., Johnson, H. C., McKenzie, D., and Mensmann, M. (2017), Teaching personal initiative beats traditional training in boosting small business in West Africa, *Science*, 357(6357), 1287–1290.

Cooper, S.Y. and Lucas, W.A. (2006), Developing self-efficacy for innovation and entrepreneurship: An educational approach. *International Review of Entrepreneurship*, 4, pp.141-161.

Elliott, S.N., Kratochwill, T.R., Littlefield Cook, J. & Travers, J. (2000), *Educational psychology: Effective teaching, effective learning* (3rd ed.). Boston, MA: McGraw-Hill College.

Fiet, J. O. (2001), The pedagogical side of entrepreneurship theory, *Journal of business venturing*, 16(2), 101–117.

Gambardella, A., Camuffo, A., Cordova, A., Spina, C. (2019), A scientific approach to entrepreneurial decision making: Evidence from a randomized control trial, *Management Science*, forthcoming.

Gibb, A. (2002), In pursuit of a new 'enterprise and 'entrepreneurship paradigm for learning: creative destruction, new values, new ways of doing things and new combinations of knowledge, *International journal of management reviews*, 4(3), 233–269.

Gupta, N. and Bharadwaj, S.S. (2013), Agility in business school education through the richness and reach: a conceptual model, *Education and Training*, Vol. 55 No. 4, pp. 370-384.

Hammond, M. & Collins, R. (1991), *Self-directed learning: Critical practice*. London: Kogan Page Limited.

Karimi, S., Biemans, H. J., Lans, T., Chizari, M., and Mulder, M. (2016), The impact of entrepreneurship education: A study of Iranian students' entrepreneurial intentions and opportunity identification, *Journal of Small Business Management*, 54(1), 187–209.

Knowles, M. (1986), *Using learning contracts: Practical approaches to individualizing and structuring learning*, London: Jossey-Bass Publications.

Honig, B. (2004), Entrepreneurship education: Toward a model of contingency-based business planning, *Academy of Management Learning & Education*, 3(3), 258–273.

Lucas, W.A. and Cooper, S.Y. (2004), Enhancing Self-Efficacy to Enable Entrepreneurship: The Case of Cmi's Connections. MIT Sloan Working Paper 4489-04, May 2004.

MISE (Ministry of Economic Development) and ISTAT (National Institute of Statistics) (2018), *Startup Survey 2016. The first survey of startups in Italy*, ISTAT.

Neck, H. M., and Greene, P. G. (2011), Entrepreneurship education: known worlds and new frontiers, *Journal of small business management*, 49(1), 55-70.

Nichols, M. and Cator, K., (2008), *Challenge Based Learning White Paper*. Cupertino, California: Apple, Inc.

Observatory Tecnológico of Educational de Monterrey (2015), Edu Trends: Challenge Based Learning, Oct. 2015, Tecnológico de Monterrey.

Oosterbeek, H., Van Praag, M. and Ijsselstein, A. (2010), The impact of entrepreneurship education on entrepreneurship skills and motivation, *European Economic Review*, 54 (3), 442–54.

Osterwalder, A. and Pigneur, Y. (2009), *Business Model Generation,* John Wiley and Sons, New Jersey.

Osterwalder, A., Pigneur, Y. Smith, A., Bernarda, G. and Papadakos, P., (2014), *Value Proposition Design,* John Wiley and Sons, New Jersey.

Owens, T. and Fernandez, O. (2014), *The Lean Enterprise: How corporations can innovate like startups,* John Wiley and Sons, New Jersey.

Piperopoulos, P., and Dimov, D. (2015). Burst bubbles or build steam? Entrepreneurship education, entrepreneurial self-efficacy, and entrepreneurial intentions, Journal of Small Business Management, 53(4), 970–985.

Ries, E., (2011), *The Lean Startup: How Today's Entrepreneurs Use Continuous Innovation to Create Radically Successful Businesses.* New York: Currency.

Secundo, G., Ndou, V. and Del Vecchio, P. (2016), "Challenges for instilling entrepreneurial mindset in scientists and engineers: what works in European universities?", *International Journal of Innovation and Technology Management*, Vol. 13 No. 05, p. 1640012.

Secundo, G., Rippa, P. and Meoli, M. (2020), "Digital transformation in entrepreneurship education centres: preliminary evidence from the Italian Contamination Labs network", International Journal of Entrepreneurial Behavior & Research, Vol. 26 No. 7, pp. 1589-1605. https://doi.org/10.1108/IJEBR-11-2019-0618

Secundo, G., Mele G., Del Vecchio P., Elia G., Margherita A. Ndou V (2021), Threat or opportunity? A case study of digital-enabled redesign of entrepreneurship education in the COVID-19 emergency, Technological Forecasting and Social Change 166(1):120565

Smith, A. and Paton, R.A. (2010), "An entrepreneurship toolkit for intensive skills development", International Journal of Entrepreneurship and Small Business, Vol. 9 No. 2, pp. 162-176.

Author Biographies

Dr. Alessandra Scroccaro is a Post Doc researcher in challenge-based learning and entrepreneurship education at the Dept. of Economics & Management, University of Trento, Italy. She received her PhD in geography and spatial management from the University of Montpellier and the University of Padua in 2012.

Dr. Alessandro Rossi is Professor of Economics and Management at the Dept. of Economics & Management, University of Trento, Italy. He received his PhD in Economics and Management from the University of Udine. He is the director of CLab Trento which organises the Startup Lab program.

Promoting Entrepreneurial, Digital and Intercultural Competences with an Interdisciplinary International Virtual Innovation Challenge

Audrey Stolze[1] Gudrun Socher[2]
[1]Strascheg Center for Entrepreneurship and Strategic Advancement Office, HM Hochschule München University of Applied Sciences, Munich, Germany

[2]Department of Computer Science and Mathematics, HM Hochschule München University of Applied Sciences, Munich, Germany

audrey.stolze@sce.de
gudrun.socher@hm.edu

1. Introduction

In recent decades, expectations towards higher education institutions (HEIs) are increasingly to generate at the same time human, knowledge, and entrepreneurial capital; hence, incorporating a third mission and becoming an entrepreneurial university. This case presents a novel international digital education format developed at the HM Hochschule München University of Applied Sciences, entitled "International Virtual Innovation Challenge". This course is the main measure of the project GlobalXChanges/Challenges (GXC), funded by the German Academic Exchange Service (DAAD) funding-line "HAW.International", from October 2019 to September 2021. This action-learning course was developed to internationalize the third mission of our university and form global citizens, by promoting entrepreneurial, digital, and intercultural competences through quadruple-helix interactions.

The curriculum design integrates global citizenship education, pedagogical processes, outcomes, and attributes (Horey *et al.*, 2018) combined with (a) the European entrepreneurship competence framework (Bacigalupo *et al.*, 2016); and (b) digital skills and competences focusing on agile project management and digital prototyping of web or mobile applications. Thus, the main goal of this novel format is to enable students to experience real problem solving in an international context, by teaching them hands-on intercultural and international collaboration competences, innovation processes and entrepreneurial thinking, agile project management, and digital prototyping. The expected outcome is to improve students' employability in modern, global, and digital work environments.

The course curriculum was developed by a computer science professor, Prof. Dr. Gudrun Socher, in collaboration with an entrepreneurship instructor from HM's affiliated entrepreneurship center, the Strascheg Center for Entrepreneurship (SCE), Dr. Audrey Stolze. The pilot edition took place between October and December 2020 and was taught by both educators in collaboration.

2. Infrastructure

The course provides bachelor students of any major with a unique 10-week action-learning experience, awarding five ECTS (European Credit Transfer System), as it was developed based on the approved module description of an existing action-learning seminar named "Real Projects", which was developed and is offered every semester by the SCE. In the new course, public governmental and non-governmental organizations propose innovation challenges that transcend national boundaries and are suitable for solutions using digital technologies. The participating students are divided into international interdisciplinary teams and follow an extended design thinking-based innovation process (Figure 1), developed by SCE, to tackle the proposed challenges and prototype digital solutions using any of the no-code tools Figma.com, GlideAPP.com, or Bubble.io.

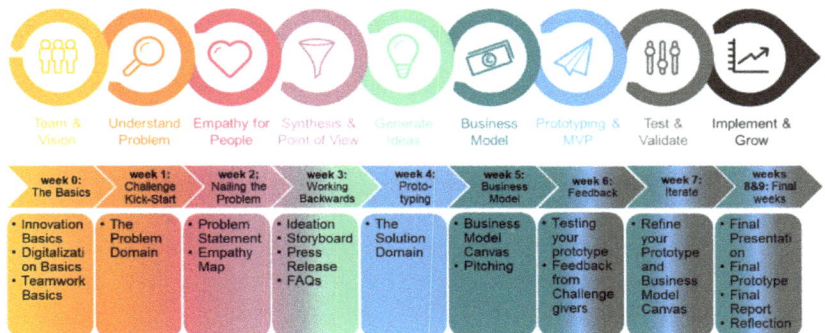

Figure 1. SCE's Innovation Process and the 10-week course curriculum

The course pilot environment included asynchronous teaching, via pre-recorded video lectures and reading material for content input (Figure 2) and synchronous teaching, through dynamic weekly live sessions with Prof. Dr. Socher and Dr. Stolze. Additionally, each student team had systemic coaching sessions with an external expert to support them to collaborate in remote international teams. Specifically, the coach supported teams with team building, project management, conflict resolution, and team reflection on the action-learning experience. Furthermore, the pilot edition also benefited from a two-part workshop (four hours in total) offered by a representative of Amazon Web Services, which supports our university's and our American university partner's cloud innovation centers. The workshop focused on ideation and production of artifacts to demonstrate the idea, based on the internal innovation process the Amazon conglomerate applies, named "Working Backwards".

Moreover, the teams collaborated through the platform GitHub. The course had an "organization" and each team had its own repository (https://github.com/gxc-international-innovation-challenge). The team repositories were private while the course was running. The students created a "wiki page" for each assignment. At the end of the course, the students launched a "GitHub Page" as part of the final documentation. For example the GitHub Page "AlpineAthletes" by Team 21: (https://gxc-international-innovation-challenge.github.io/AlpineAthletes-Team-21-/). After the conclusion of the course, the teams' repositories were published open access.

3. The Learning Outcomes and Stakeholder Perceptions

The pilot edition had innovation challenges proposed by three partner organizations that were tackled by ten international interdisciplinary student teams (table 1). Forty-one students from eight countries participated in the pilot edition. Most students were full-time Bachelor students from three of our strategic partner universities in the USA, Finland and Austria. Among the students most study computer sciences, information systems, or an engineering field, (63%), 7% are undertaking a management-related degree, and the remaining students (30%) were from other degrees (anthropology, political sciences, physics, agriculture, biomedicine, and others). Furthermore, 44% identified as female students.

Figure 2. Course Structure on the Learning Management System

At the end of the course the three partners – Municipal Labour Department, the German Ski Federation, and the Youth Association – received a 3-page case report describing the challenge results and containing links to the prototyped solutions. These reports are published open access on https://www.hm.edu/en/international/projects_1/gxc/gxc_virtual_innovation_challenge.en.html.

Table 1: Innovation challenges and prototyped solutions

Partner Organization	Innovation Challenge Proposed	Student Team Solutions
Labour Department of the Munich Municipality	How can municipalities, through digital solutions, motivate local companies towards climate protection, in times of crisis?	4 Teams worked on the challenge. The first team prototyped a user-friendly mobile and desktop carbon footprint calculator that allows companies to easily visualize their CO2 consumption, compare their CO2 consumption with other companies of their size and sector, and receive recommendations for how to reduce their CO2 emissions. The second team prototyped a website that provides businesses with information and resources to build green walls in office spaces. The third team prototyped a user-friendly carbon dioxide tracker that generates graphs of a business' progress in CO2 reductions. Based

Partner Organization	Innovation Challenge Proposed	Student Team Solutions
		on their progress to carbon dioxide neutrality, businesses receive different 'Ecolabels'.
		The fourth team prototyped a ranking system of small businesses according to their reduction of CO_2 emissions, giving consumers a way to shop at businesses that are working to be more eco-friendly.
German Ski Federation	How could we digitally connect/engage ski enthusiasts in a way that adds value to all stakeholders and leads to an active and interconnected ski community?	Three teams worked on this challenge.
		The first team prototyped an app that connects winter sports enthusiasts in a competitive and fun way with the opportunities to win prizes via a fantasy winter sports league.
		The second team prototyped an app that enables people to purchase any kind of ticket related to snow activities – from making a reservation in a restaurant to ski rental reservations.
		The third team prototyped an app that enables ski enthusiasts to find and connect with other skiers who have common interests and be part of a community to exchange information and advice.
Youth Association Kreisjugendring Munich Branch	The future of youth participation: How to empower the youngsters?	Three teams worked on this challenge.
		The first team prototyped an app that allows the youth association members to exchange information via chat and vote in decision-making processes.
		The second team - inspired by the usability of the dating app 'tinder' - prototyped an app that allows young people to find their perfect event or activity, fitting to their needs and wants, by swiping through offers from different associations/clubs in their city.

Partner Organization	Innovation Challenge Proposed	Student Team Solutions
		The third team prototyped an app for global young citizens to connect across borders, engaging in online discussion forums, polls, virtual workshops, and events related to societal and environmental causes they care about.

The 41 students who took part in the pilot evaluated the course positively, agreeing the virtual environment was suitable for the course's purpose, as the instructors' engagement and energy provided an enriching learning experience that enabled students to collaborate effectively in international interdisciplinary teams. For instance, one student summarized her learning experience saying, "I like the intercultural aspect of the course, and that the professors were extremely personable, which made it easy to talk to them. The professors and challenge givers gave great feedback, which was very helpful in our process. The live sessions were structured well, and I especially liked getting to talk to people that were not in my group. I also liked my team members, which made it enjoyable to work on the project". The most valued aspect was the learning provided through the virtual teamwork experience. Students increased their network and improved their intercultural communication skills. The main difficulties they faced were due to time differences, as most teams had members with up to 10 time zones apart. Only four students reported team conflicts, which caused them to worry during the course. Nevertheless, these did not negatively affect their individual grading.

The innovation challenges provided students with a real-life meaningful experience, in which they felt to contribute towards something that could be implemented in the future by the partner organization. Thus, students reported having improved their entrepreneurial skills, as they experienced working with a variety of tools and resources introduced during the course, as either part of the agile project management, or the innovation process. In this regard, a student reflected, "I love the course itself and its overall setting, to be in an international team with other students from around the world. I also like that we were able to experience prototyping for a real-life challenge with a team, where nobody knows each other before. I think that is a really valuable experience for the future in my career. The coaches being there for us and having weekly sessions with them was really helpful".

Figure 3 shows a comparison of the students' perceived development of their entrepreneurial mindset thanks to their participation in this pilot. The European Project Astee (Moberg et al., 2014) has developed the survey based on the Entrepreneurial Competency Framework. We compared the results with those of two other student cohorts who joined initiatives from our institution. One is a massive open online course "Introduction to Entrepreneurship", which is a self-passed asynchronous learning experience. The second is a "Real Projects" seminar, which was taught by Dr. Stolze, in English, to a group of international students. The key differences of this "Real Projects" seminar to the pilot are:

(a) This was a block-seminar, placing 5ECTS in a single week,

(b) it took place in person, weeks before the pandemic started,

(c) it did not have partner organizations engaging, and

(d) it had a stronger emphasis on business modeling and startup creation in the field of EdTech (education technology).

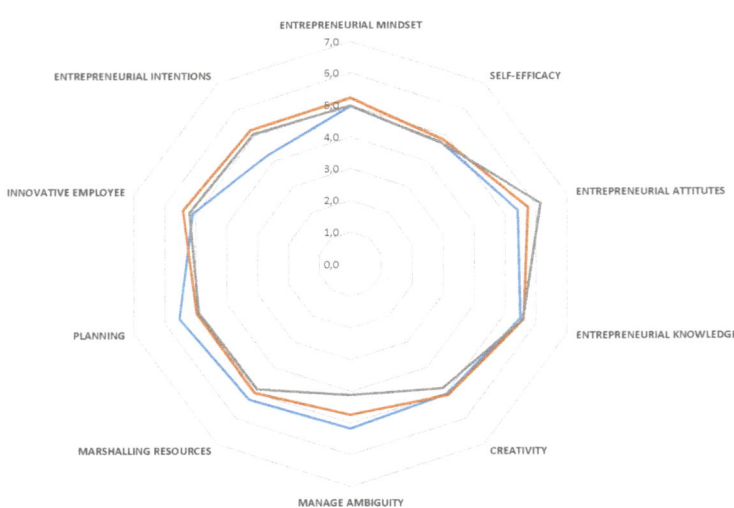

GXC Pilot in Blue (n=26); MOOC in orange (n=279); and Real Project EdTech in grey (n=16).

Figure 3. Entrepreneurial Mindset Survey Results

Overall, we observe that the course format enabled the students to improve their abilities to plan, to manage ambiguity, and to marshal resources to a higher degree than the other two formats. This is most likely due to the emphasis placed on agile project management and the action-learning experience of working on an interdisciplinary international remote team. The pilot did not improve students' entrepreneurial intentions and attitudes at the same level as the other two courses. This might be because the other two courses did not have partner organizations and all student teams position as startups, while at GXC teams could choose to position themselves as a startup team developing the solution or as an innovation-as-service team delivering the solution to the partner organization, who they viewed as their client.

Moreover, considering GXC's goal of third mission internationalization, it is important to also view the perceptions of other relevant stakeholder groups (Table 2) regarding the pilot edition.

Table 2: Stakeholders Perceptions of Pilot Edition

Stakeholder Group	Summary of stakeholders' perceptions of the pilot (Retrospective)
Partner Organizations	Partner organizations expressed appreciation for the opportunity to take part, expressing they received relevant insights to foster internal discussions in their organizations.
	They demonstrated engagement and enjoyment for having the opportunity to engage with young adults from different nationalities during three virtual live sessions. One organization's representative regarded it as "refreshing". Overall, partner organizations were positively impressed by the professionalism shown by the students in their interactions.
	All three partners after the conclusion of the pilot received a case report published open access sharing the team's prototyped solutions.
	All three partners took internal actions based on the pilot's results. The Municipality aims to integrate one solution of a team to improve networking and data visualization of an ongoing sustainability program for small and medium-sized local companies. Another organization is currently discussing with potential contractors the development of a mobile application merging functionalities of two of the prototyped solutions. The last partner organization is currently looking for funding opportunities to finance the development of a mobile application inspired by the teams' prototypes.
	One partner organization has joined the second edition, which has a topic-focus on sustainability issues in the sports industry, with an

Stakeholder Group	Summary of stakeholders' perceptions of the pilot (Retrospective)
	innovation challenge that should support the development of their sustainability strategy.
International Partner Universities	Partner universities representatives recognized the GXC team's efforts to enable international collaboration among the students in a time of travel restrictions. The finish partner university motivated by this effort also enabled our universities to join one of their summer programs remotely.
	The course quality and action-learning format were acknowledged, with a representative of the American partner affirming: "I believe MUAS has really set the bar for what a high-impact and meaningful virtual international program can look like so I am very excited to be part of this program's launch!"
University Leadership (Vice-presidents and Chief Strategy Officer)	The pandemic meant most staff had to focus on "core activities". The fact that the project team did not wait to iterate GXC into a digital format, taking immediate action was positively evaluated.
	University leadership was particularly interested and satisfied with the pilot's results, emphasizing the value delivered by the synergies promote among different initiatives of the university to enable agile transformation.
	The agile transformation and timely approval of the new measures by the steering committee and the DAAD meant GXC returned less than 10% of the 2020 budget allowance to DAAD, which is an average return rate even in 'normal times'.
	The resources developed by GXC are re-usable and can be adapted for online action-learning seminars in different contexts, as international project management, innovation and entrepreneurship, and mobile application. All content-videos produced are hosted on the university streaming server and accessible to all professors and lecturers who would like to integrate them on their courses (e.g. embedding it on Moodle courses).
	GXC is seen by the university leadership as a "success case story" with lessons learned to be shared internally. The team was invited to present the case in an internal board meeting and at an event for international partner universities.
	Lessons learned reported provided insights for the development of the university's new third mission internationalization and all members of the GXC management team were invited to contribute to a strategy co-creation workshop.
	The sustainability of GXC's outputs and lessons learned beyond the funding period are key aspects to be addressed by the team after the pilot. The synergies created with other projects and formats could improve the chances of the project's sustainable continuation post-funding.

4. The challenges

The initial scope of GXC included 2-week and 4-week students' international exchange with our four key strategic partner universities in Austria, Switzerland, Finland, and the United States. However, the unforeseen pandemic of 2020 directly affected international mobilities. In March 2020, our university was days away from receiving the first American incoming exchange students when all measures were forcibly canceled. In a matter of 2 months, the new virtual format was developed and the program's advisory board and the DAAD approved all changes as new measures.

Reflecting on the transformation process, the GXC manager concluded: "our team's entrepreneurial mindset enabled us to manage the chaos, and the collegiality, respect and trust existing among the team members definitely made things a bit lighter. Running the pilot was a fun experience". This entrepreneurial mindset is clearly justified by the fact the team followed effectual thinking principles, transferred insights and lessons-learned from past initiatives, built upon existing resources and capabilities in the meso-level and generated synergies among pre-existing formats across the university. The transformation process is described in the ECIE2021 full paper entitled "Third mission internationalization in times of travel restrictions through digital transformation: the role of dynamic capabilities and effectual practices".

5. Future Plans

The course had a second edition in Spring 2021 (March-May 2021) and it will be offered again in the Fall (October-December 2021) as a measure of the GXC project, which extended its funding period from DAAD until December 2021. Next, the SCE will incorporate all developed resources into its entrepreneurship teaching and make it available to all HM's departments and professors, who collaborate within the seminar format "Real Project". For instance, all video content is available on HM's streaming service in open access to be re-used and shared (https://mahara.hm.edu/view/view.php?id=31409). Additionally, Dr. Stolze expects to continue teaching a course with the same format of the "International Virtual Innovation Challenge", as an international virtual edition of the "Real Projects" seminar, focusing on digital transformation challenges presented by public and private partner organizations.

Another opportunity for future development emerges from the fact that this course, as a "Real Project", counts 5 ECTS towards the HM Certificate in

Entrepreneurial Thinking and Acting (15 ECTS). This certificate is currently only offered to HM students, but the new course opens up the opportunity to internationalize it and offer it to all incoming exchange students and other international students. The certificate is composed by a 2 ECTS self-paced MOOC (massive open online course) offered in English, a "Real Project" seminar (5 ECTS), an internship at a startup (5 ECTS) and a final report (3 ECTS). Within the GXC program in Summer 2021, HM students will be able to do 1-month fulltime international virtual internships at early-stage Startups located outside Germany who are part of the international acceleration program eBridge Alliance (https://www.sce.de/international/ebridge.html), initiated by the SCE/HM. This format can be also offered to international students who might do internships (virtual or in person) at early stage startups located at the SCE/HM incubator, enabling them to fulfill all requirements to be awarded the HM Certificate Entrepreneurial Thinking and Acting.

The case of GXC and its International Virtual Innovation Challenge action-learning course exemplifies how to internationalize an HEI's third mission initiative and promote global citizenship, by combining entrepreneurial, digital, and intercultural competences as learning outcomes. The pilot results are reassuring, as the main stakeholders involved positively assessed it. The pilot effectively promoted students' Critical Global Citizenship, as it combined "Thought" and "Intention" with "Action" (Hartman and Kiely, 2014), enabling students to express their desire to take action and make a difference. After all, ultimately, the purpose of HEIs, in the context of 'entrepreneurial societies', is to ensure that its citizens thrive in their endeavors (Audretsch, 2014).

References

Audretsch, D. B. (2014) 'From the entrepreneurial university to the university for the entrepreneurial society', Journal of Technology Transfer, 39(3), pp. 313–321. doi: 10.1007/s10961-012-9288-1.

Bacigalupo, M. et al. (2016) EntreComp : The Entrepreneurship Competence Framework, Publication Office of the European Union. doi: 10.2791/593884.

Hartman, E. and Kiely, R. (2014) 'A critical global citizenship', in Crossing Boundaries: Tension and Transformation in International Service-Learning, pp. 215–242.

Horey, D. et al. (2018) 'Global Citizenship and Higher Education: A Scoping Review of the Empirical Evidence', Journal of Studies in International Education, 22(5), pp. 472–492. doi: 10.1177/1028315318786443.

Moberg, K. et al. (2014) How to assess and evaluate the influence of entrepreneurship education - A report of the ASTEE project with a user guide to the tools.

Acknowledgements

The authors are thankful for the support and engagement of the Head of SCE Prof. Dr. Klaus Sailer, Lars Schmitz from Amazon Web Services, Prof. Dr. Patricia Arnold, Prof. Dr. Nicole Brandstetter, Prof. Dr. Anke van Kempen, Prof. Dr. Sonja Munz, Dr. Sven Winterhalder and Andrea Schramm.

The German Academic Exchange Service (DAAD) funds the GXC project with funds from the German Federal Ministry of Education and Research.

Author Biographies

Dr. Audrey Stolze is Head of Entrepreneurship Research at Strascheg Center for Entrepreneurship and international program manager at Hochschule München (Germany). She received her Doctoral degree from University of Hohenheim (Germany) and graduated in business management from Hochschule Osnabrück (Germany) and Universidade Feevale (Brazil). She worked in Brazil, England and Germany with market research, international business development and founded two startups.

Prof. Dr. Gudrun Socher is a full professor at Hochschule München and head of the Munich Center for Digital Sciences and AI (Germany). She worked at tech companies including Yahoo!Inc. in the US and Germany. She holds a Ph.D. from Bielefeld University (Germany) with research at the California Institute of Technology and graduated in computer science from KIT Karlsruhe (Germany) and Grenoble University (France

www.ingramcontent.com/pod-product-compliance
Lightning Source LLC
Chambersburg PA
CBHW060836170426
43192CB00019BA/2800